Development
Economics

Development Economics

Economics

Searching for the Roots of Rural Income Inequality

M. Riad El-Ghonemy

Development Economics:
Searching for the Roots of Rural Income Inequality

Includes bibliographical references and index.

Printed in the United States of America by CreateSpace
7290-B Investment Drive
North Charleston, South Carolina 29418

For additional information visit www.riadelghonemy.com

ISBN: 1516860977
ISBN 13: 9781516860975
Library of Congress Control Number: 2015913220
CreateSpace Independent Publishing Platform
North Charleston, South Carolina

CONTENTS

To my daughter, Samira

LIST OF TABLES

FOREWORD
By Gary Carr, PhD

The catchphrase "The rich get richer and the poor get poorer" is more than a line from an American popular song of the 1920s. It has long been shorthand for the effects of economic inequality and a criticism of the free market system. And here, it is the essence of Dr. M. Riad El-Ghonemy's book *Development Economics: Searching for the Roots of Rural Income Inequality*.

Dr. El-Ghonemy documents and presents examples of how, despite the efforts of global experts to "eliminate" the poverty and ill health of the rural poor, the process is most often bogged down in red tape and conflicting government and corporate goals. He draws these examples from his career of more than fifty years as a developmental economist, working with a score of international organizations such as the World Health Organization, the Organization for Economic Cooperation and Development, and a half-dozen United Nations agencies and other organizations sporting initialisms such as USAID, FAO, IFAD, ILO, IMF, CAPMAS, ESCWA, and WCARRD. He serves as a lifetime senior associate at the Department of International Development at Oxford University.

Dr. El-Ghonemy is a well-trained, well-schooled social scientist; a numbers person; and a stickler for details. But he also brings a longer vision to his work, a passion for pointing out the flaws in any system that makes things worse for those whom the philosopher Frantz Fanon called "the wretched of the earth." He writes from firsthand knowledge of the effects of various land-reform programs over the decades on those on the lowest rung of agrarian society.

M. Riad El-Ghonemy was born in 1923 into a farming family in rural Egypt, in the village of Delingat. Because the family owned their land, they were considered middle class. His father was a civil servant employed in land management. Delingat was a two-hour drive from Cairo. The village had no electricity, running water, or sewerage—public services that would not appear until the 1960s.

Shortly after El-Ghonemy's birth, his father moved the family to Cairo, although he spent his summers with his grandparents in Delingat, where he remembers diving off the backs of buffalos into the canal with his cousins. At age five, he began his education at the local madrassa. After two years, he passed the entrance exam for Mounira Primary, one of the best government schools in Cairo.

After Mounira, he went on to study agricultural economics at the University of Cairo. There, his major extracurricular activity was founding the Fellah (Peasant) Society in 1942. His motivation was to create awareness among his fellow students about the problems of poor people in rural areas and to understand the economic and institutional factors causing gross inequality and poverty among the *fellaheen* (peasants).

After his graduation from the University of Cairo in 1944, he was appointed to the school's Land Tenure Studies Section, where he conducted field studies on hired agricultural workers, the poorest in rural Egypt. At that time, he wrote that these studies revealed how a relatively small group of domestic and foreign capitalists, including some members of the royal family, formed a coherent system of control of the land and capital markets, not only in rural areas but also in all economic activities through the multiple roles they maintained: membership in Parliament and on boards of directors of banks as well as sugar and cotton industries.

For the next two years, he continued with the Fellah Society as well as working on studies of rural household income and expenditure with the International Labour Organization (ILO). Then, in 1950, he was accepted to study for a master's degree in agricultural economics at the University of Tennessee at Knoxville. After that, he moved on to North Carolina State University in Raleigh.

The twenty-seven-year-old Egyptian was comfortable with the academic side of America, and although he spoke perfect English, it was British English, a foreign tongue in the American South. Having long since survived the childhood "banana incident" described in chapter 1, he looks back with amusement at an exchange between Arthur, his office mate, and himself over the location of the restroom:

I asked, "Where is the WC?"

His cool answer was "There is no WC around here. It's a hundred kilometers away." When he noticed my insistence and astonishment, he added, "Do you want to go to the WC from the first day? Relax, boy. I have been here for two years, and I have never been to the WC." The language problem was solved by Arthur after I repeated my question. He explained to me the puzzle: *the WC* was an abbreviation for the Woman's College in Greensboro, which periodically organized dances with the agricultural economics department's students. (At that time the students at the Raleigh campus were all male!)

After earning his PhD in 1954, El-Ghonemy studied land economics at several other US schools, among them the universities of Chicago and Wisconsin.

In 1955, he returned to Egypt, where his task was to establish criteria for resettling six thousand farmers from the overpopulated Nile Delta to newly reclaimed land near Alexandria.

In 1959, he was appointed by the UN Food and Agriculture Organization (FAO) to study recent land-reform issues in Cuba, and he attended a meeting with President Fidel Castro, who explained the objectives of the Cuban land-reform policy, among them, "liberating" sharecroppers and landless workers from the power of absentee landowners who owned large tracts of land. El-Ghonemy discovered that pre-Castro inequality was manifested in the fact that only 9 percent of the total number of landowners owned 73 percent of Cuba's arable land.

Between 1983 and 1992, with grants from the FAO, El-Ghonemy studied the effects of land reform in eight central African countries, among them Uganda and Kenya.

He found that under centuries-old land-tenure systems, the land had been communally owned by indigenous groups (tribes, families, and communities). These groups devised sets of working rules for land rights (use and occupancy) and subsisted by grazing and cultivating food crops when rain permitted. Furthermore, he argues that anthropologists and geographers recognize this customary socioecological system as suitable for land use and livestock husbandry in a semiarid climate. It has been the cornerstone of food security for millions of indigenous people and, in turn, their social security. El-Ghonemy finds this age-old system invaluable, as it provides employment to the pastoralists' family members within a rational division of labor between women and children, resulting in the production of a considerable part of the countries' total meat, milk, wool, and hides and the conservation of their key natural resource, pasturelands. He writes about the trend toward privatization as follows:

It is ridiculous that some foreign professionals still see this customary system as nothing but backward or primitive and in need of being privatized according to the conventional Anglo-Saxon conception of efficiency in agricultural production by way of individual private ownership of land linked to the capital market. Despite existing strong arguments for maintaining customary land tenure, and in spite of a lack of empirical evidence on the production superiority of individual private land ownership over customary tenure arrangements, privatization policy is pursued with vigor in most African countries. It is also enforced in spite of empirical evidence that customary tenure is compatible both with the production of export crops and with food production.

The experience of several privatizing countries suggests the following:

1. The vulnerability of individual owners to the loss of land to urban speculators as well as to mortgage and heavy indebtedness
2. The weakening of women's customary rights in land and command over food
3. The shift away from food crops toward cash/export crops (coffee, cocoa, etc.)

Moreover, El-Ghonemy finds that, because of high transaction costs, the land buyers are mostly businesspeople, politicians, senior civil servants, members of the armed forces, and owners of large amounts of land. These nonagricultural land speculators know the law and registration procedures, and they have contacts with credit institutions, land surveyors, and other bureaucrats. Financially, they can afford the costs of surveying, registration, and issuing private title deeds.

He writes that the primary effect of privatization on rural well-being is increasing insecurity, in terms of both the loss of household command over food and the loss of customary rights to land. In Malawi between 1986 and 1990, the area of customary land that was privatized doubled. Land buyers converted the production of food crops into burley tobacco, and former small landholders became wageworkers and net buyers of food. With the population growing fast, at 3.7 percent per year, food production per person fell rapidly. In contrast, tobacco production had increased more than 50 percent by 1991.

In Uganda, the economic policy reform toward export-led growth has facilitated shifting land use from grazing and growing food (cassava and millet) to commercial ranching managed by urban land buyers who have kinship relations with influential policy makers. The buyers erected fences around their ranches, depriving pastoral households in the surrounding areas of traditional corridors used for their own passage and the grazing of their animals.

From his findings in the Darfur region of Sudan in 1984, El-Ghonemy saw the roots of what would surface as a major agricultural/political disaster twenty years later. He found that, in a scheme for bringing in settlers to cultivate pastoral land, "many of the Sudanese settlers had no experience in growing cotton and groundnuts which they were obliged by the government to grow."

Time and again, El-Ghonemy confronts the same issues of the market economy being imposed on a traditional socioeconomic structure, making things worse for the many and lowering them deeply into poverty and poor health. Once in a while, he finds a country like South Korea in the late 1950s, where extensive redistributive land reforms combined with government regulations have enabled the market mechanism to gradually function effectively.

Throughout this book, El-Ghonemy continually presents evidence of the harm done by the few to the many by the imposition of a market economy, whether it fits or not. Nevertheless, the scientist and analyst in him contends, like the detective in the old US television series *Dragnet*, that these are "just the facts, ma'am, just the facts."

Whether land-tenure reform is politically feasible under certain power structures is not for the social scientist or the development analyst to judge. What he or she can do is use the faculties and professional tools to understand the totality of rural underdevelopment problems in a specific situation; to point out their implications for poverty, equity, economic growth, and conflicts of interest; and to suggest alternatives.

In his books *The Political Economy of Rural Poverty* (1990) and *The Crisis of Rural Poverty and Hunger* (2007), he attempts to clarify a common misinterpretation of "for" or "against" government intervention and "pro" or "anti" market approach *without* specifying the tactics for poverty-reduction focus and the nature of the government's role. Moreover, he says, "It is equally unhelpful to make a generalized policy preference between 'market-based' and 'state-based'…land reform *without* placing the debate in a *country-specific* agrarian context." One size does not fit all.

But what comes out of *Development Economics: Searching for the Roots of Rural Income Inequality* most clearly is El-Ghonemy's passionate belief in land reform as the key to alleviating poverty in agricultural societies, and that an unchecked market economy is not the answer. His experience, gained over six decades, has yielded scores of answers to the problem. Rather, what is needed is to select the right solution for the particular case, along with the will to implement it.

PREFACE

Written between 2010 and 2014, the narration of events in this book is intended to share the lessons learned from personal and professional experiences with lifelong friends, university colleagues, and students. It presents the driving forces, defining events, and memorable personalities shaping my career in the field of development economics. In this account, I may have overlooked other events or a few people, and the reader may not agree with my judgment on the relative importance of these events.

Nevertheless, I have detailed three narratives about events that have made marked changes in my development-related thinking. They are not presented in the order of their importance, because they are closely linked and are interdependent.

The first is my parents' decision to move from my birthplace, Delingat, a poor rural community in the Nile Delta, to Zein el-Abideen, a crowded working-class area of the religiously conservative Sayeda Zeinab district of Cairo. At that place, I received my elementary, primary, and secondary education.

The second defining event is my travel in 1950 to start my four-year scholarship grant for doctoral studies in the United States and to write my dissertation on land reform and economic development at North Carolina State University–Raleigh.

The third influential event is in the professional field: my field studies and work with governments in the Middle East, Latin America, and Africa. Notable were the African field studies in eight poor countries during 1992, which directed my mind to the real meaning of poverty and hunger, and to the deficient aggregation of the poverty-stricken Congo, together with Brazil and Indonesia, in a single category of nations—the so-called "developing countries." Irrespective of their historical and social structural variations, analytical tools derived from the experiences of rich industrial countries were applied, and sweeping generalized judgments on poor countries' developmental problems were made by Western donor countries and international agencies, with a standard policy prescribed.

Throughout this account, I have confined the presentation to the focal point of events and analytical concerns shaping my development-related thinking and providing the type of work that enables me to assist developing countries. My efforts have focused on both fieldwork and writing toward poverty alleviation and participation of the poor in the process of development in their communities. Consequently, important personal events are excluded.

Before concluding this preface, I wish to highlight the analytical concerns arising from my long participation in the examination of development problems of poverty and gross inequality that have made me a development economist with a mission to assist governments and nongovernmental organizations in poverty alleviation. These are the concerns on which the discussion is based:

The first concern is the neglect of institutions and their determinants within a historical context. For example, in agricultural land-tenure arrangements, which determine the allocation of resources, production incentives, income distribution, and power structure do not receive the necessary attention. In my book *The Political Economy of Rural Poverty* (1990), I made an attempt to examine these relationships based on empirical studies with an emphasis on institutional monopoly. Similarly, the developmental effects of inequality of opportunity for access to basic needs and productive assets, primarily land in the rural economy, deserve special examination. For instance, I have found that in the Philippines, the policy makers' emphasis has been on growth and *not* the broad objectives of development economics. Accordingly, multinational corporations were welcomed, with their priority on foreign capital for labor-saving technology to produce mechanized luxury goods at the expense of the peasantry's food crops.

My second analytical concern is the confusion over the roles of the market and the state/government in economic development. The confusion is loaded with value judgments and discernible bias, resulting in the use or misuse of terms having a wide range of meaning. For example, private property being the foundation of capitalism, and its transaction via the market regulated by the state in the case of rents and mortgages, has been protected.

Alfred Marshall, the founder of modern economics, wrote, "Taking it for granted that a more equal distribution of wealth is to be desired, how far would this justify changes in the institution of property, or limitation of free enterprise?" (1952, 41). The institution of property in the sense used by Marshall is taken to mean the intangible or the exchangeable rights in ownership and use of property as determined by law or custom. This content of property is distinct from physical property. It denotes leasing, sharing arrangements, indebtedness, and mortgage, as well as inheritance and mortgage regulations for the transfer of property rights from one generation to the next. This exchangeable content of property rights also denotes security of tenure and property-based power or political advantages—that is, a landless poor is politically dominated by landlords and has no power in community decision making.

In addition, this content of property rights determines both the flow of accrued income and its distribution among the participants through the interaction with market transactions (e.g., Adam Smith's famous reference to "the invisible hand" that stimulates production and distributes gains between participants in the exchange process). Also, the exchangeable rights induce or inhibit investment in improving the productivity of the physical content of property by way of technical change (such as irrigation and soil improvement by applying fertilizer) and, therefore, affect the intensity of land and labor use.

If our interpretation of Marshall's notion is correct, the question is, should these rights in private property be preserved on the grounds that property and economic freedom are sacrosanct irrespective of their distributional effect, or should they be conditioned by the state power with a view toward maximizing social welfare?

This question has engaged the interest of many philosophers and analysts from different strands of economics. In his *Wealth of Nations* (1776), the prudent Adam Smith conceived a principle governing the role of the state protecting, as far as possible, every member of society from the injustice or oppression of every other member of it (Book IV, 651). This principle implies that the state exercises its political power to restrain the economic freedom of individuals or corporations that abuse such freedom for attaining private gains at the expense of others. In his scholarly argument, W. J. Baumol says, "I believe that the politician is, in many cases, justified in taking, and indeed forced to take, action on many (practical) problems: perfect analysis or no" (1965, Part II, 204-07). In fact, this is what governments are doing.

Private property, despite being the central bond of capitalism, has aroused public concern over the consequences of institutional monopoly manifested in the concentration of landownership in a few hands combined with growing landlessness, chronic indebtedness of the peasants, and eviction of tenants. These manifestations are among the proximate causes of persistent rural poverty, and they can threaten political stability.

When the balance of power swings toward the interests of poor peasants and landless workers, the state intervenes to condition the institution of property rights and, in varying degrees, to limit the economic freedom of entrepreneurs in agriculture. In this quest for justice, the state in a capitalist system does not abolish the concept of private property in land but instead regulates ownership rights and rectifies market defects in the rural economy. The state, or its executive branch, the government, supports the operation of the market mechanism (e.g., the land and credit markets) in many ways, including by issuing laws to protect property rights, and fulfills business ethics in land mortgages as well as banking and trade operations.

The extent of state intervention in private-property market economies is unlimited, as expressed by Friedrich Hayek, the 1974 Nobel laureate in economics: "All governments affect the relative position of different people, and there is under any system scarcely an aspect of our lives which might not be affected by government action" (1986, 81).

I hope this book might inspire the many students who would probably judge some elements of my achievements and shortcomings and who, I trust, would strive for a better standard for meeting development challenges in the years to come. I hope they will appreciate my antipoverty ideas and work and continue the work that I started when I was nineteen to twenty-one through the organization of the Fellah Society in 1942, while studying at the University of Cairo. In realizing this hope, they would be interested to learn that the world's poor and hungry are estimated in 2010 at 1.3 billion people, having increased by a hundred million in one year since the 2009 estimate.

ACKNOWLEDGMENTS

I am indebted to the following colleagues at Oxford University's Queen Elizabeth House for their kind assistance during the preparation of this book: Penny Rogers, Denise Watt, Wendy Grist, and Gary Jones.

The appearance of this book resulted from several contributing factors. The first is the careful word processing by Zainab Usman. The second is the kind assistance received from Mastan Ebtehaj, the librarian of the Middle East Centre, St. Antony College, University of Oxford. I would like to recognize my son Anwar for his abiding interest in the subject of this book and its publication and Dr. Gary Carr for his editorial counsel. Lastly, my wife, Marianne, has patiently read some drafts and has put up with my long absence from home.

To all these kind people, I am most grateful.

M. Riad El-Ghonemy
Queen Elizabeth House
Department of International Development
University of Oxford

LIST OF ABBREVIATIONS

ARTEP	Asian Regional Team for Employment Promotion (New Delhi)
CAPMAS	Central Agency for Statistics (Cairo)
CPI	consumer price index
ESCWA	United Nations Economic and Social Commission for Western Asia (Beirut)
EU	European Union (Brussels)
FAO	Food and Agriculture Organization of the United Nations (Rome)
GDP	gross domestic product
GNP	gross national product
Ha.	hectare = 2.4 acres
HDI	human development index
IBRD	International Bank for Reconstruction and Development (World Bank, Washington, DC)
IFAD	International Fund for International Development (Rome)
IISS	International Institute for Strategic Studies (London)
ILO	International Labour Organization (Geneva)
IMF	International Monetary Fund (Washington, DC)
MNC	multinational corporation
NGO	nongovernmental organization
ODA	Overseas Development Administration (London)

OECD	Organization for Economic Cooperation and Development (Paris)
OPEC	Organization of Petroleum Exporting Countries (Vienna)
PPP	purchasing power parity
UAE	United Arab Emirates
UNCTAD	United Nations Conference on Trade and Development
UNDP	United Nations Development Program (New York)
UNESCO	United Nations Educational, Scientific and Cultural Organization (Paris)
UNFPA	United Nations Fund for Population Activities (New York)
USAID	United States Agency for International Development (Washington, DC)
WCARRD	World Conference on Agrarian Reform and Rural Development (Rome)
WHO	World Health Organization (Geneva)

CHAPTER 1

THE RURAL ORIGIN OF A DEVELOPMENT ECONOMIST

1.1 Growing Up in a Community Deprived of Basic Public Services

An important landmark of my father's birthplace, Gabaris village, is the shrine of my two great-grandfathers, surrounded by a paved space and a wall, within which the present male generations of the El-Ghonemy clan assemble, pray, and break the fast on the last Friday of the month of Ramadan. Accompanied by my brother Mohyee, I regularly take part in this annual family ritual. At the assembly in 2014, 160 male members of the El-Ghonemy clan gathered from distant places.

From my participation in this annual assembly, I could observe six common characteristics: most of the elderly had made the pilgrimage to Mecca and are called *Hajj*; a notable increase in the number of university graduates; the absence of family fragmentation and, thereby, two generations living in a single household; the lack of interest in or motivation for holding political positions, including parliament memberships; being part of the agricultural land-based middle class; and higher social ranking because of being *Ashraaf*, meaning "descendants of the Prophet Mohammad."

My father Riad attended the village *kuttab* (elementary school) in the early 1900s, learning Arabic, the Quran, and arithmetic. In 1918 he married his cousin Sayeda Hindy. According to a long-established custom, both my father and mother were tattooed: my mother on her chin and my father on his wrist. When I asked my mother how painful the tattooing was on the sensitive skin of the chin, she replied that it was culturally based and that it was a prevalent custom; she had no choice, and it had to be done, like girls' circumcision, which was later prohibited in the entire country for hygienic reasons.

I was born on the cold night of January 24, 1923, at my grandfather's home in Delingat village. I spent the winter months of January and February with my mother and grandmother in a room heated by a mud-built oven outside one wall, where bread was baked, water was heated, and food was cooked. A few meters outside in the house's open yard was the noisy manual underground water pump next to the *zeer*, which was used for keeping and cooling drinking water. A *zeer* is a large jar made of special clay and placed on a stand one meter above the ground, beneath which is a smaller jar to collect the filtered water. At that time, there was no piped, purified water or sewage system in Delingat, like the rest of rural Egypt. Public services, together with electricity, were introduced during the 1960s and 1970s, resulting in major changes in rural life, ranging from satellite televisions to refrigerators, notably in households whose sons worked in the oil-rich Arab countries.

The guest quarters and the family sitting room were separated from the yard by a covered passage leading to the main house entrance. On the arrival of unexpected guests, my grandmother used to push the geese around, causing them to be noisy and implicitly conveying to the guests her message that the new arrivals would not be staying for lunch or supper!

My mother and my elder cousin Labib liked to tell me about the customary celebration of my birth, since I was the first boy in the Riad family. They told me that on the occasion of my reaching one week in age, my grandmother made a loud noise by banging a heavy brass bowl. The purpose was to stimulate and activate my sense of hearing, a different practice from that followed by my father when he first saw me in Delingat: he whispered some verses from the Quran into my right ear. Whatever the wisdom of both practices, I never had any trouble with my ears, and I still, in my nineties, enjoy perfect hearing.

In these conditions and at the accommodations of my grandparents, I spent three weeks with my mother and grandmother until the arrival of my father from Cairo to fetch me and my mother. After a five-hour journey by the village taxi, the Alexandria railway line train, and then a Cairo taxi, we reached our newly built two-story house in the Sayeda Zeinab district, where I spent twenty-seven years of my childhood and early adulthood, until my travel to the United States.

1.2 From Madrassa to North Carolina

At the age of five, I began my preprimary education at the Sheikh Ali Madrassa. It was a choice of family convenience: the school was a five-minute walk from home, and Sheikh Ali was my father's companion at the local Zein el-Abideen mosque. But Sheikh Ali was unpopular among the pupils in his one-class all-boys school because he carried a long bamboo stick with which he disciplined us. He taught Arabic, arithmetic, and the Quran. After two years, I passed the competitive entry exam for Mounira Primary School, one of the best government schools in Cairo, well known for its teachers' notable record and vast sports fields. The school was, however, nearly two kilometers away from home, in the district of upper-middle-class residents and close to Garden City, the residential district of Egypt's pashas (lords), where many embassies are located and most diplomats live.

On my first day of school in the dining room at Mounira, I was faced with an embarrassing social-class-system problem of using a fork and knife for the first time. We did not use them at our home or in Delingat village. When I tried to peel a banana with the fork and knife, the boy sitting next to me shouted, "Look how this peasant boy peels the banana."

I was upset, and at home, I explained to my parents what had happened. My mother comforted me, while my father said, "You must challenge that boy in the classroom." At the end-of-year exam, I was one of the top two pupils in the class and was rewarded by joining twenty other top-class performers in a school trip to Alexandria. This incident, which happened when I was seven, had a lasting effect on both my personal life and my professional writing: a defiance and the desire to challenge in response to a demanding and difficult situation.

Another memorable event in my primary-school days was the administration of the antibilharzia injection daily for a period of ten days during two school years. When the school bell rang announcing the arrival of the school doctor, I went to have a urine test, and the results proved that I had bilharzia (schistosomiasis). It caused my bladder to bleed from an infection by parasites living in contaminated Nile water of the irrigation canals. I had caught the disease by swimming and diving from the backs of buffalos into the canal with my cousins during the three-month summer vacation in Delingat. During those vacations, I was also infected with another endemic disease, trachoma, which caused swollen eyelids and corneal scarring. It was transmitted by flies and from using other infected people's objects. This illness infected me several times and has required constant treatment, resulting in my sight being weakened permanently.

I remember my struggles to learn English at Mounira Primary School. The boys of Sheikh Ali's Madrassa and my cousins at the village amused themselves by asking me names of things or actions in English. Those who went to primary schools and learned some English used to challenge and embarrass me in spelling difficult words, a situation that has influenced me to master the spelling for writing my books and other publications. In fact, I realized that spelling in English is the most difficult of my learned languages: Arabic at the age of five; English at the age of seven; French at secondary school; Spanish for the qualifying exam of the doctoral degree in the United States; and Italian during my initial six-year residence in

Rome, working with the Food and Agriculture Organization of the United Nations.

Another lesson I learned was to avoid gambling. One day, while walking home from the Mounira School carrying my heavy book bag, I crossed the bridge over the Cairo-Helwan railway line. I stopped at the end of the bridge because I was attracted by a crowd watching a man demonstrate how to play cards for money. It was the first day of the school week, when my father used to give me five Egyptian piastres as my weekly pocket money. I could not resist the excitement of putting my five piastres on top of a card that was placed facedown. The game seemed to be very simple: if my guess about the card number was right, I would be paid double its amount. But the whole thing proved to be a clever trick, cheating a seven-year-old schoolboy, and I lost my weekly pocket money. My immediate reaction was to cry, and at that moment the school's arithmetic teacher was passing by. He stopped and forced the card-playing man to return my money; otherwise, he would call the police. I got my five piastres back, but the teacher painfully pinched my ear, telling me, "Do not do that again, and I won't inform the school headmaster or tell your father."

To this day, I have neither played cards nor gambled, and I have always—in my writings and teaching on income distribution—called for the support of earning *primary* income, from owned assets such as property and through lawful means, and spoken against the accumulation of *secondary* income from bribes, cheating, and other corrupt practices.

Two other boyhood experiences stay with me even today. The first was when I learned for the very first time about Egyptian Christians or Copts (*al-Aqbat*), as two of my close classmates were Copts. It is through them that I learned to respect other beliefs, a principle that is laid down in the Quran. The second was during a school trip to the section on the history of rural life at the Agricultural Museum in Cairo, when the teacher explained to us the living conditions of the farming population during the Pharaonic period nearly five thousand years ago. I was captured by the fact that the house layout and farmers' customs at that time were nearly the same as those in the Delingat village where I was born.

When I finished my four-year primary education, my father was appointed as administrator of the sixteen-thousand-acre Royal Estate at Kafr el-Sheikh, a rural province in the north of the Delta to which my family moved and where we lived for five years. The nearest secondary school was forty kilometers away in Mahalla al-Kubra, to which I commuted daily by the rural Delta train.

Kafr el-Sheikh was a rice-growing area infested by mosquitoes that transmitted malaria during the summer. Twice I fell ill to the disease. At the Mahalla School, I joined the school Boy Scouts and was introduced to camping, self-discipline, and helping others in need. I used the two-hour daily journey by the Delta train to study and do homework. One market day when the train was overcrowded by people and livestock, I had with me my Boy Scout uniform, which my mother had ironed and wrapped in a newspaper (at that time there were no plastic bags). On my arrival at Mahalla to join the Boy Scout parade, I discovered that the goat standing in the aisle next to me on the train had chewed through the parcel containing my uniform and had eaten the entire shoulder of my shirt. I was dismayed, but I had to be in the parade because I was the drummer.

The Mahalla School did not have the educational facilities for teaching the important fifth and last year of secondary education. My father decided to move me to Cairo Banba Qaden secondary school, which was well known for having a small student body but high educational standards and was financially supported by the Royal Estates Department, where my father had worked. It also had widely recognized teachers of English and French with extensive experience in their home countries—the United

Kingdom and France, respectively—and in teaching young members of the royal family, such as Prince Farouk and his sisters.

Unfortunately, I suffered during this important year from two diseases: malaria, which reoccurred since I had lived in Kafr el-Sheikh, and a very painful eye infection. Consequently, I was unable to achieve the 1940 secondary school certificate's high level required for entering the school of medicine at the University of Cairo, which was my father's wish for me. Even so, my level was good enough for my second choice, to study agricultural economics at its college of agriculture. There I met Dr. Ahmad Hussain, the professor of agricultural economics who was my mentor during my early career, and from 1940 he had a lasting influence in shaping my development interests.

At the college, Dr. Hussain was the supervisor of the Fellah Society, which I organized in 1942, with its aims and field activities attracting several students. The driving force behind its organization was my astonishment at the contrast between the many highly trained academics who had graduated from top British universities, on the one hand, and the illiterate masses of working people at the college farm and messengers (*farrasheen*) on the other. I also thought that the share of technology and pure science (e.g., genetics, soil chemistry, bacteriology, entomology, and the physics of water for irrigation) was excessive, whereas the study of rural living conditions and the understanding of the poor farmers' problems were almost absent. The motive for organizing the Fellah Society was to create awareness among the students about the problems of poor peasants and rural areas. During the university summer vacation, the Fellah Society's members were engaged in voluntary rural-development activities in their own villages, primarily combating illiteracy, and in assisting the peasants in demanding better government health and education services for their communities.

1.3 Confronting the Real Development Problems

As the director-general of the government's Fellah Department, Dr. Hussain arranged for some members of the Fellah Society and me to visit and practice fieldwork in the pioneer rural-development centers established in 1940. The purpose was to have an understanding of the economic and institutional factors that caused conditions of gross inequality and poverty among the *fellaheen* (peasants). He also arranged for me to broadcast twice in Egypt's official radio program *The Fellah Corner.* The subject was the role of the youth in providing voluntary rural-development work during their summer vacation. Soon after my graduation from Cairo University in 1944, Dr. Hussain appointed me to a position in the Fellah Department's Land Tenure Studies Section, where I conducted, under his guidance, field studies on hired agricultural workers being the poorest in rural Egypt, farm tenancy arrangements, and peasants' annual income and expenditure. The studies revealed how a relatively small group of domestic and foreign capitalists, including some members of the royal family, formed a coherent system of control of the land and capital markets. They controlled a wide range of economic activities through the multiple positions they maintained: membership in Parliament and on boards of directors of banks as well as sugar and cotton industries.

In early 1950, I was chosen to work with the International Labour Organization (ILO) in conducting a rural household income/expenditure survey in a sample of fifteen Egyptian villages, the results of which served as a basis for instituting Egypt's Social Security Programme, initiated by Dr. Ahmad Hussain when he joined the cabinet as Egypt's minister of social development in May 1950.

In addition to field observations that were accumulated during the summer vacation in Delingat and Gabaris villages, my field studies conducted while working in the Fellah Society exerted a powerful influence upon my graduate studies for the master of science and PhD degrees. They also had a strong influence upon my perception of development economics in general, rural poverty, social stratification, and the case for redistributive land-reform policy in particular.

An illustration may help emphasize this point: I did a study in 1948 of the migratory agricultural workers (*taraheel*) in Kafr el-Sheikh province and conducted a survey of some 2,700 landless agricultural households with the support of two ILO international experts in 1950. My 1948 study indicated the widespread disinvestment in human agents, whereby the workers live unsheltered in the fields where they worked or on the banks of the canals, drinking directly from the infected Nile water of the irrigation canals. Nearly half of them were younger than fifteen years old, missing school and joining the masses of illiterate rural people. In the latter households survey, conducted by using a minimum household net income of thirty-five Egyptian pounds in 1949–50, the rural poor in Egypt were identified and estimated: 1.06 million hired agricultural workers, 27,000 sharecroppers, 214,300 holders of less than one acre (*feddan*), 150,000 pure tenant-cultivators of one to two acres, 30,000 family heads of nomadic population, and 30,140 disabled heads of families, making an estimated total of 1.5 million poor households who were all illiterate. By using a uniform average of five people per family, I arrived at a total of 7.7 million poor people, which represented 56.1 percent of the rural population in 1950; nearly 80 percent of the males and 92 percent of the females were unable to read and write.

In March 1950, the daily newspapers announced the list of two hundred government scholarships and called for the submission of applications. The list included one scholarship to the United States for studying rural economics, and I applied for it. One month later, I was informed that I'd been accepted to study at the University of Tennessee, Knoxville, for a master's degree and at North Carolina State University for my doctoral studies in agricultural economics. I learned later that my work in the Fellah Society and my voluntary summer work on illiteracy alleviation and serving poor peasants during summer vacation were given special consideration in my selection, together with the recommendation from Dr. Hussain.

The formalities for my travel to the United States were complex. Most importantly were the American consulate's requirements for granting visas only after receiving satisfactory medical reports. This was a difficult task, costing medical expenses and four months' labor commuting between Cairo clinics to obtain medical certificates confirming my complete recovery from trachoma, bilharzia, and malaria. By the end of May 1950, I'd met all the requirements and was granted the visa for study under the supervision of the Egyptian Education Bureau in Washington, DC, which was asked to arrange for the periodic medical checkup during my four-year graduate study in the country. The US embassy in Cairo attached to the visa a sealed letter labeled "Only to be opened by the New York Airport's Medical Officer."

It was a long air journey, since the plane was powered by four propellers (jet engines were not used for commercial airliners then) and had to stop in Athens; Rome; Paris; London; Shannon; Greenland; Newfoundland, Canada; and Boston before reaching the final destination of New York. The journey took thirty-two hours but was very exciting and comfortable, primarily because I traveled first class, paid as part of my scholarship, by the Egyptian Ministry of Education for the entire trip until I reached the university campus. Being served by a glamorous young hostess and the chief steward made me feel more important than just a postgraduate student from Delingat village. Nevertheless, I missed the goats and the crowds on the Mahalla rural train. A memorable event was the five-minute inspection by the chief medical officer at the New York airport. He opened the sealed letter written by the American consulate in Cairo and gazed at me. My immediate thought was that he was going to send me straight to Cairo. To the contrary, he said, "I am very impressed that after being ill twice with bilharzia, malaria, and trachoma, you are fit to come in order to get your doctoral degree."

I traveled by train to Knoxville, where I was met at the station by a postgraduate student from the Department of Agricultural Economics. I immediately experienced the language difficulty, arising from his American accent with a strong southern drawl. My host said to me, "Well, what do you know?" My confusion enhanced his explanation. "I mean, how are you, and how was the trip?"

After my successful nine-month study at Knoxville, I was qualified for a master of science degree in agricultural economics from the graduate school of the University of Tennessee, and the title of my postgraduate thesis was "A Study and Analysis of Farm Tenancy in Egypt." One week later, I went to Raleigh, North Carolina, for my studies toward a doctorate.

On my first day in Raleigh, I was given an office to share with Arthur Mackie, whom I asked, "Where is the WC?"

His cool answer was, "There is no WC around here. It's a hundred kilometers away." When he noticed my insistence and astonishment, he added, "Do you want to go to the WC from the first day? Relax, boy. I have been here for two years, and I have never been to the WC." Here again, a language problem was solved by Arthur after I repeated my question. He explained to me the puzzle: *the WC* was an abbreviation for the Woman's College in Greensboro, which periodically organized dances with the department's students. (At that time the students at the Raleigh campus were all male!)

1.4 Investigating the Root Causes of Poverty in Rural Egypt

After completing my PhD studies, I spent two weeks each at the University of Chicago and the University of Wisconsin at Madison, the home of the Land Tenure Study Center. In addition, I visited the University of Mississippi at Jackson and Louisiana State University in Baton Rouge. The purpose of both visits was to understand the universities' work on tenancy and sharecropping arrangements in the cotton- and rice-growing areas, which had institutional conditions similar to those in Egypt.

During my doctoral studies in North Carolina, I was encouraged to go with friends to distant places, like New York and Miami, during long holidays. In the summer of 1952, I went to Myrtle Beach in South Carolina. There, I saw firsthand the meaning of racial segregation, which was widely practiced in the South. It was clearly indicated at the entrance to the beach by two arrows pointing in opposite directions: one for the "whites," and the other for "coloreds" or "blacks." Courageously, I entered the white section and was politely served by a young white American, who fixed the umbrella and its table for me. In New York, I visited Professor Charles Issawi at Columbia University, who was a pioneer analyst of the political economy of Egypt. He made an original study of the large landowners of Turkish origin who refused to marry other Egyptians, except from their own social-class rank.

During these travels by car, an incident occurred at a drive-in cafeteria on my way to Miami. While I was having a cup of coffee, a young American man sitting next to me and drinking beer asked, "Where are you from?"

"Please guess," I said.

His guess was wild: it ranged from Brazil to Turkey to India. After unsuccessful attempts, he asked again, "Where the hell are you from?"

"Egypt," I quickly answered.

His response was, "What's the difference between Brazil, India, and Egypt—all damn underdeveloped countries."

After completing my doctoral studies, I departed from Raleigh, and finally from the United States, by sea from New York to the Mediterranean port of Alexandria. En route, we stopped at the Italian port of Naples. There, I was shocked by the relative poverty in contrast to the affluence in New York; there were lots of beggars asking for money and cigarettes. I realized it was the consequence of the long fascist rule of Italy, followed by the Nazi occupation at the end of the Second World War, until the liberation of southern Italy by the American and British forces. In addition, that region suffered greatly from gross inequalities, particularly the concentration of land in a few hands. Also disturbing was the power of the Mafia, still going strong after seven hundred years. The Mafia had originated in Sicily, headed by big landlords to serve their private interests through extortion, blackmailing, and ransom payments. (As my career progressed, I would discover this control over the land by powerful interests continuing, but by more subtle and legal means.)

Later in 1958, when I visited the Italian south—accompanied by Professor Mario Bandini, the director of Italy's Institute of Agricultural Economics, who was actively engaged in the implementation of the 1952–53 Italian land reforms in La Sila and the rest of the Calabria region in the south—I was impressed by the poverty-alleviation efforts but disturbed by the continued sociopolitical influence of the Mafia.

The arrival back home on the liner was as exciting and dramatic as the departure from Cairo four years earlier. When I landed, I was met by my parents, four brothers, my sister and her husband, and four of my former colleagues in the Fellah Society.

CHAPTER 2

DEVELOPMENT ECONOMICS
IN OPERATION

2.1 Examining the Impact of Land Reform and Industrialization on Rural Egypt

After two happy days with the family, I went first to the Fellah Bureau that became a part of the Social Development Department of the Ministry of Social Affairs and then to the Agrarian Reform Agency (ARA) of the Ministry of Agriculture that had been recently instituted to implement the agrarian-reform law of September 1952, finding myself amid the jungle of Egyptian bureaucracy. My thoughts were focused on meeting the challenge of converting the academic principles I had learned in the United States at the Egyptian government's expense into practical programs to help the *fellaheen* and other poor groups who were given priority in the development policies of Gamal Abdul Nasser's revolution in July 1952.

Before and during my studies in the United States, I had direct contact with Mr. Sayed Marei, the president of the ARA, who expressed interest in the subject of my doctoral dissertation on land reform and economic development in Egypt. When I presented him a copy, he asked me to assist his office staff in understanding the economics of land redistribution and arranged field visits to several land-reform areas. I welcomed the opportunity to have direct communication both with the peasants who became new landowners and with the ARA field staff implementing the reform program. But I was confronted by the bureaucratic attitude of the senior administrators in the Social Development Department and the ARA. The situation was complicated further by my invitation to deliver lectures and give seminars at the newly established Ain Shams University in Cairo and the University of Alexandria. Thanks to the kind intervention of Mr. Marei, the administrative difficulties were surmounted during 1954–56 and resolved for good by my release from the Egyptian government in March 1957 to work with the FAO of the United Nations, first in Rome and later in Latin America.

For investigating the impact of land reform, I suggested to Mr. Marei a monitoring system to be followed by the ARA in conducting field studies starting with the villages of El-Mansheya, Gabaris, Inshas, Itaiy al-Barood, and Mat'ana, the results of which were updated and analyzed in my 1990 book, *The Political Economy of Rural Poverty*. The book pointed out the higher land productivity of several crops in land-reform areas than in non-reform areas, owing to the intensive production services provided by the cooperative societies in the reform areas. The results of these field studies indicated also the smallness of the farming units allotted to the new owners in 1952 (one hectare, or 2.4 acres) and remaining constant while their household size increased from six to nine on average, suggesting an absolute need for providing the beneficiaries with nonland assets, notably education, livestock, and labor-intensive rural industries. These proposals were accepted by Mr. Marei and implemented at Inshas as a pilot scheme.

At that time, planned land settlement in newly reclaimed lands after the construction of the Aswan High Dam was a prominent issue, for which my assistance was needed. In 1955, I established the criteria for selecting the six thousand new settlers from densely populated areas in the Delta and helped in the implementation of this comprehensive project in Abis near Alexandria.

These field studies showed the limited scope of the land reform, which redistributed only 14 percent of Egypt's total cultivated land to peasant families, representing only 9.6 percent of the total agricultural households in 1965. This partial scope, combined with Egypt's Malthusian situation of continued population pressure on the scarce cultivable land, left nearly 40 percent of the total agricultural households as landless, wage-dependent workers. These large groups were the poorest in rural Egypt, according to the results of my study with the ILO team of experts.

In April 1960, I participated with Dr. Haloul, professor of rural sociology at the University of Alexandria, in designing a field study and training the Rural Development Department's field staff to determine the impact of the cotton-textile factories in the Kafr el-Dawar agricultural areas southeast of Alexandria. The goal was to record the living conditions of a random sample of 809 households living in the villages near the textile factories. The results of the study showed that only 18 percent of the total sample (144 households) were born and lived in these villages *before* industrialization, whereas 82 percent were migrants who came between 1935 and 1940 from distant villages, 36 percent of whom were engaged—before migration—in agricultural activities (landless workers and small tenants). Interestingly, the study indicated that, twenty years after migration, only 15 percent of the migrant households continued working in agriculture. The rest shifted to industry and supporting services, compared with the national average of 71 percent of the total population working in agriculture in 1956. The low proportion of 15 percent of the migrants working in agricultural activities deserves some explanation. It indicates the significant changes introduced in the social, economic, and occupational status that were brought forth by industrial activities in the studied sample area of rural Egypt. The results and policy proposals of this field study were formally presented to senior officials in the Egyptian Ministries of Planning, Industry, Social Affairs, and Agriculture.

2.2 Assisting Developing Countries in Poverty Alleviation

A. Afghanistan, Middle Eastern, and North African Countries

I received a short letter in March 1955, from Dr. Rainer Schickele, chief of the Land and Water Use Division of the Food and Agriculture Organization of the United Nations (FAO) in Rome, the agency that initiated my international field experience, which lasted twenty-six years. In that letter, he kindly praised my analysis of economic-development issues in my doctoral dissertation, a summary review of which he had seen in the *American Journal of Farm Economics*. He asked me to work with the FAO as a land-tenure expert, after the receipt of a written consent from the Egyptian government. The task was to conduct a field study on land-tenure problems and related policy issues in the FAO's Near East region, the results of which were to be presented to a meeting of government representatives at Salahuddin in northern Iraq in October 1955.

I welcomed the opportunity and agreed with Dr. Schickele to visit Afghanistan, Iran, Iraq, Syria, Sudan, and Turkey to compile necessary country-specific data on the subject of the regional meeting. I also collected basic material for writing a paper and presented the results of its analysis for discussion at the same meeting. The title was "Income Distribution and Capital Formation in Relation to Land Reform Programmes in the Near East." An updated version of the paper was published later in the United States in *Land Economics* (1968). My involvement in rural studies in the Middle East continued intermittently over the next twenty-five years.

Afghanistan

My FAO field mission to the region began in April 1955 by visiting Afghanistan, a poor agrarian economy that depended completely on agriculture for its food, employment, exports, government revenues, and production of raw materials for cottage industries. Its poor economy lacked such basic data as population and agricultural censuses, as well as the absence of land-ownership surveys (Cadastral surveys) and publications on land tenure and the rural population. What existed were merely estimates made by government officials, particularly those in the land-tax departments.

The population of this landlocked country in 1955 was estimated at twelve million, mostly nomads and seminomads. The state held the property title to most land cultivated by insecure tenants—when rainfall permitted. Secure legislative rules on land-property rights were nonexistent. The senior officials of the Royal Afghan Government and village heads (*walis*) did not find it necessary to change the existing agrarian system, except the development of limited areas of state-owned land through irrigation schemes, whose purpose was the settlement of the nomadic people. This attempt at ending their nomadic lifestyle took place—with financial aid from the United States—in the Helmand River area of six hundred thousand acres, where the newly settled were charged with growing cotton and orchards and raising livestock.

I did not see any quick prospect for secure access to productive land for the millions of the poor nomads, landless workers, and sharecroppers whom I interviewed in 1955 and who told me that they regularly listened to their radios to the neighboring Soviet Union's propaganda on communist ideas and Marxian principles.

My next field studies for the FAO were to Iran, Libya, and Yemen, the summary of which is presented below, suggesting, in contrast to Afghanistan, that they had adequate information on their agrarian system and had already initiated public actions to improve the living conditions of their peasants.

Iran

In Iran, my study shows that, in 1951, the Shah distributed 240,000 acres of his Pahlavi Estates to 8,300 farmers at a reduced land price. The farmers' production and marketing needs were served by the newly established Bank Omran and its network of state-controlled agricultural cooperatives. Privately owned large farms were *not* affected at that time; however, during my subsequent visits in 1962 and 1966, I learned that the state issued land-reform laws that redistributed an area of privately owned land representing 22 percent of the total cultivable land and benefitting 38 percent of the total agricultural households. Moreover, in his study of the 1969 law, Abdolall Lahsaezadah of Shiraz University reported in 1993 that the law took nearly three years to implement, and by then 738,119 peasants had purchased their holdings. In addition, 61,805 tenants bought from ex-owners their less productive land, but at a higher price than that established by the government.

Libya

The account of the development problems and antipoverty policies in the Middle East would be incomplete without recounting what I learned from my six-year involvement (1961–67) in the design and implementation of the large-scale project "The Development of Tribal Lands and Transformation of Nomadism to Settled Farming in Libya." In a historical context, the pastoral nomads of Libya represented 57 percent of the total agricultural population in 1960, and the tribes held communally 40 percent of the total area of the cultivated land. A few years before my 1961 field study, Libya was ranked a poor country by the World Bank, which estimated per capita income at only fifty US dollars and described its economy as "dependent on the exports of sheep, goats and wool," (Higgins 1959, 3).

These features of underdevelopment are rooted in a long foreign occupation of the oil-rich Libya; first was the Ottoman rule for nearly four centuries, followed by the Italian occupation of 1911–42, and the British and French joint rule until Libyan independence in December 1951. After the discovery of oil-rich deposits in 1959, the revenue to the government multiplied five hundred times to reach $30 million in 1961.

Subsequently, I presented to the Libyan government my proposed project for permanently settling the nomadic people in the former Italian farms, with technical assistance provided by an FAO multidisciplinary team of international experts. The entire project was financed by the Libyan government, which allocated 17 percent of its total oil revenue for it. Most of the allocation was spent on infrastructure, particularly for bringing groundwater to the beneficiaries' farm units of five to ten acres each and for the financing of all public services.

My discussion with senior government officials in 1961 revealed that the plentiful and sudden flowing of oil revenue caused them little or no concern about economic conditions. It soon became apparent that lavish public spending could not quickly transform tribal-based rural communities, with their recent nomadic background, into technology-using farmers and institutionally viable farming systems.

The remarkable investment in human capital in terms of advanced health, education, housing, and sanitation services had raised the rural people's standard of living in general and their quality of life in terms of literacy, infant mortality, nutritional status, and so on. However, a political expediency of lavish spending on housing, contrary to my advice of enlisting the participation of the new Libyan settlers in the design of houses to suit their tribal values and customs, took place. For example, I noted in 1967 that in the Jabal al-Akhdar area, the new settlers were reluctant to live in the costly government-built houses with concrete roofs, even at no cost to them. Instead, they preferred to live in the tents that they set up next to their houses.

I have dwelled at length on the six-year Libyan experience in the transformation of nomadism to settled farming because it raises interesting questions with regard to both the economics of development and the balanced/unbalanced development in countries experiencing sudden, plentiful, and rapidly flowing oil revenue.[1]

Yemen

In 1981, I was appointed by FAO (Rome) and UN/ESCWA (Beirut) as a leader of an international mission to Yemen. The task was to examine the country's program and produce projects to improve the land-tenure system and rural living conditions. Let us start with my studies of several Middle Eastern countries, the results of which were presented to the meeting in north Iraq.

Yemen is a predominantly agriculture-based economy. In 1980, agriculture employed 75 percent of the total labor force. The then-current development strategy stressed economic growth *without* emphasis on equity issues, including the improvement of the land-tenure system and the regulation of the powers of the owners of tractors and irrigation water pumps. The defective land-tenure system showed up in the results of the 1981 agricultural census: one-fourth of the distribution of landholding sizes was less than half an acre each, making up only 1.5 percent of the total cultivated land and mostly fragmented into three to nine pieces each. On the other hand, the large landholders' category of ten acres and more represented only 8 percent of the total number of landholders, yet they owned 55 percent of the total land.

---

1 For a clarification of the ambiguous concepts of balanced and unbalanced development, there are different emphases on *what* is balanced or unbalanced: the power between public and private sectors; the power of trade unions and the state; economic and technological development in capitalism combined with cultural, social, and human development; high spending and savings; exports and imports, and so on. See, for example, Michael Novak, *The Catholic Ethic and the Spirit of Capitalism*, New York: Free Press, 1993; and Kaeran Gazdar, *Germany's Balanced Development*, chapters 2 and 3, London: Quorum Books, 1998. See also my discussion on rural-development strategy for Yemen and Sudan in this volume.

The resulting inequity of Yemen's economy was also characterized by three features.

The first was the low quality of life in rural areas, where infant mortality was 158 per thousand and life expectancy was only thirty-nine years. Illiteracy was high, at 75 percent among men and 95 percent among rural women, and 10 percent of students enrolled in secondary education were female.

The second was the increased migration of male rural workers to neighboring oil-rich Arab countries, which subjected the economy to great uncertainty with regard to remittances amounting to 53 percent of total income (gross domestic product).

The third was the prevalence of integrated rural-development (IRD) projects that were financed by different donors, each having different priorities and interpretations of IRD without a clear direction by the government. The result was utter confusion, fraught with experimentation and the dispersion of the scarce resources. What was alarming indeed were the objectives and criteria used by these projects' donors: they focused on internal rate of return while artificially boosting the foreign-exchange component of projects and *not* giving priority to the effective participation of rural people in rural-development activities. A different focus might well have led to the alleviation of gross inequalities and absolute poverty.

Based on these areas of concern and on the findings of my field studies in the Yemen's West Khawian and Tehama, I prepared poverty-oriented actions and discussed them with the deputy prime minister; the ministers of agriculture, social affairs, and planning; and the chairman of the Central Planning Organization. These policy actions are presented in the following section.

My Proposed Strategy for Yemen's Development in 1981

The strategy included targeting benefits to small farmers, the landless workers, and the disadvantaged rural women. It also included

1. a pilot project for the Khawian area with a joint financing by the FAO and the Islamic Development Bank;
2. the setup of a national coordinating committee for rural development to pool and coordinate different ministries' work and resources as well as the establishment of socioeconomic rural-development indicators for 1980 to serve as a benchmark for monitoring future progress; and
3. giving special attention to rural women, who became heads of households in the absence of their husbands working in neighboring oil-rich Arab countries. This responsibility was added to their load of farming and child care. Staggering rates of illiteracy among women (98 percent of total women fifteen years and over) and the absence of schools for vocational training were so endemic that women were excluded from national statistics on workers' economic activity.

The Complementarity between Government Intervention and Market Forces: The Case of the Middle East

Guided by the principles of Rawls's *Theory of Justice* (1972) and Baumel's *Theory of the State* (1965), I have emphasized the *complementarity* (not *either/or*) between government intervention to enable the land and capital markets to reduce poverty, increase productivity, and achieve food security. The purpose behind my emphasis on the complementarity was my reaction to the World Bank's and the International Monetary Fund's neoliberal ideology in their aggressive approach toward the heavily indebted poor countries suffering from foreign debts. In 1984–85, these poor countries agreed to implement the World Bank and the IMF's prescribed structural adjustment and financial-stabilization programs attached to severe clauses in contractual agreements for debt relief.

Briefly, these clauses include cuts in budget deficit, devaluation, privatization of the public-sector economic establishments, and tax reform. The debt-relief agreements put little emphasis on the distributional effects and poverty reduction. Instead, they favored the single ideology of private-property capitalism with little or no government intervention, particularly the redistributive land policy.

Eight Middle Eastern countries accepted the World Bank and IMF prescription and its attached clauses, none of which helped the rural poor or the country as a whole.

First: The Case of Egypt

1. Average annual growth of the GDP fell from 8.8 percent in 1973–83 to 2.6 and 2.5 percent in 1985 and 1986, whereas gross domestic investments, budget deficits, and national account deficit improved slightly.
2. Real wages, subsidy payments, and shares of health and education spending in total government expenditure worsened.

Second: Contrasting Development Policy in Iraq and Sudan

In 1986, I addressed a series of seminars at Cornell University in which I contrasted development policy between oil-rich Iraq and poor Sudan.

The economy of the Sudan remained overwhelmingly agricultural, employing 75 percent of the total workforce, whereas industry employed only 5 percent. Furthermore, the results of the labor surveys suggested rising inequality between urban and rural sectors and within agriculture, owing to the government wage policy and its generous subsidization of the wealthy mechanized farmers. In addition, these rich farmers encroached into grazing areas, which poor pastoral nomads use to move from one pasture area to the next.

To illustrate the rising inequality in the Sudan during the 1970s, average public investment in the wealthy mechanized sector was almost forty times as much as investment in the traditional poor sector. Most affected were the landless workers whose employment was seasonal and uncertain because of rainfall instability, repeated droughts, and the long civil war in the resource-rich south. Accordingly, food insecurity prevailed, with nearly 40 percent of Sudan's food consumption being imported and mostly given in grants. In addition, reliable estimates suggest that absolute poverty was massive, ranging between 70 and 80 percent.

With regard to Iraq, I also addressed the following question: In a country endowed with large amounts of oil, natural gas, and sulfur, and with abundant cultivable land and water resources, why had illiteracy, poverty, and inequality prevailed? This state of underdevelopment of the otherwise rich Iraq prevailed because of three major factors:

1. Substantial resources were allocated to militarism since a bloody coup d'état in July 1958.
2. Development priorities were distorted in terms of military expenditure. As a percentage of Iraqi national income, such expenditures rose from 7 percent in 1960 to 30 percent in 1986.

3. Political instability resulted from three military coup d'états and eighteen different governments having different ideologies during the 1960s.

Likewise, militarism was manifested in extravagant imports of sophisticated arms, the value of which reached one quarter of the total country imports; these were used in military conflicts with the Kurds in the north, the Kuwaitis in the south, and Iran in the east. This state of policy making resulted also in an average military spending per person reaching more than double the average spent on education and health combined in 1981. Such a scale of distorted public spending and the country having its priorities set by military governments were facilitated by the sharp rise in government revenues from oil and gas, which contributed 90 percent of the total export earnings.

Third: Examining the Effects of the 1980s Economic Reforms on Rural Poverty in Syria

The results of the 1994 agricultural census of Syria tell us that the number of landless workers in agriculture has doubled in number since the 1970 census. Rural poverty is concentrated in *muhafazat* (provinces) Al-Hasaka and Deir El-Zor. Such prevalence of poverty is confirmed by the results of the two household income/expenditure surveys of 1996 and 2004. Using the lower poverty line established by the government, I estimated the extent of poverty at 46 percent of the total poor who lived in the muhafazat in 2004, and most of them were landless agricultural wage-dependent workers.

Fourth: Exploring Development Problems in Egypt, Libya, Morocco, Tunisia, and Sudan

During the period 1992–93, I found out from my field studies and discussions with policy makers, local-level officials, and farmers that despite a wide variation in development problems and policy, the poor fellaheen were unable to fulfill their expectations, owing to the following defects:

1. Many of these policies were used by politicians to pacify the discontented poor farmers without harming the interests of large farmers. Hence, the momentum for genuine rural development created by the political environment in the 1950s and 1960s was dissipated.

2. Red tape and cumbersome bureaucracy constrained both implementation and effectiveness of the programs.

3. The lack of residence-allowance payments for local officials tempted some of them into corruption, principally those working in collecting taxes and those working in state farms and village cooperatives.

4. Development imbalance has been built into the governments' plans and programs. Invariably, total output growth and *not* human well-being (health, education, food security, and poverty reduction) is given absolute priority in development objectives. Hence, I pointed out to government officials the distorted monitoring system followed in judging progress, including the statistical system used. Added to price intervention, public capital and current expenditures have yielded an imbalanced development with a substantial transfer of surpluses from the rural agricultural sector to other sectors of the economy. For example, governments devoted a disproportionately large share to support the internationally uncompetitive and indiscriminately protected manufacturing industry. Any surpluses extracted from rural areas were also used to subsidize consumption in urban areas—where most bureaucrats live. Hence, the resulting rise in greater rural-urban income inequality was probably unintended.

5. In this process of development imbalance, the absolute priority given to industry has neither adequately absorbed a sufficient number of the labor force nor increased correspondingly the share

of manufacturing industry in total gross domestic product and exports. Despite increased rural to urban migration, the rural agricultural labor force relative to industry has remained quite large, except in Libya and Tunisia.

6. The imbalance criteria used in this analysis placed Tunisia at the top of the development experience and Sudan at the bottom. By absorbing labor at an annual rate of 3.7 times as much as agriculture, industry in Tunisia reduced the pressure of rural people on land. Keeping the numbers of agricultural laborers from swelling thereby improved the productivity, income, and nutrition per person of rural people remaining on the land. The opposite took place in the Sudan and Morocco, where resources devoted to protected industries were disproportionately high, to the disadvantage of investment and employment in the rural agricultural sector.

Despite the government proclaiming pro-fellaheen rural-welfare policy, I found out during my field studies the following two major economic-development issues:

1. The masses of low-income rural people had no say in or control over the design of rural-development strategy and programs, and they are not to blame for the resulting defects and imbalanced development. Policies were made by a small group of army officers after coups d'état (Egypt in 1952, Libya in 1969, and numerous coups in Sudan).

2. Backed by an increasingly sizable bureaucracy, extensive government intervention in the agricultural sector has occurred by way of imposed and overstaffed cooperatives at the village level. Such cooperatives were given a wide range of tasks: implementation of agrarian-reform programs and the allocation of land among crops. These institutions were also used by governments as an employment outlet for less qualified young graduates, while the fellaheen became powerless because they found themselves dependent on

what local government officials decide. Furthermore, trade unions in agriculture were either banned or government controlled, and their right to strike was prohibited.

B. Latin American Countries

My interest in the development issues of the Latin American countries started by learning Spanish during my postgraduate study. There, I also met students from that region with whom I shared my opinion on the defects of land-tenure systems and gross inequalities in rural areas. The opportunity to travel and work in Latin America came in March 1957 when I was reappointed by the FAO of the UN to work at its headquarters in Rome.

After three months behind a desk, I expressed to Dr. Schickele, the division director, my preference for moving away from office work (dealing with generalities on land policies within a bureaucratic environment) to work, instead, with a farm population at a country level. Behind this preference was the desire to assist governments and their field staff in understanding the role of land tenure in shaping their economies and their social structure, with the view toward resolving the peasants' problems. I stressed the welfare objectives of the FAO—that "the first cause of hunger and malnutrition is poverty"—and that therefore the FAO should help countries "in the survey of existing systems of land tenure for the purpose of identifying changes that promote the welfare of rural workers."[2]

Paraguay

My first fieldwork in Latin America started in Paraguay in October 1957 as an FAO land-reform expert. Once again, I encountered some amusing communication problems in Paraguay, where the people speak two languages: Spanish among the educated and the Indio dialect (*Guarani*) of the indigenous inhabitants. On the first day after my arrival at Asuncion from Rome, I practiced my knowledge of Spanish at the hotel dining room. For breakfast, I ordered the usual European bread, butter, marmalade, and

---

2 Readers wishing to learn more about FAO responsibilities for tackling both land-tenure problems and poverty in rural areas may read El-Ghonemy, *The Political Economy of Rural Poverty*, introduction and part 1, 1990.

eggs. The waiter was astonished when he heard me asking for *burro*, or "butter" in Italian, and he called the chief waiter, who explained the puzzle to me: *burro* is the Spanish word for "donkey," and in Paraguay they had instead *lomito* (beef) for breakfast, which is the ordinary morning meal for farmers. Afterward in the hotel shop, I wanted to purchase some postcards and asked whether there were better ones than what I was shown. The man in the shop, like the waiter before him, was astonished because I had wrongly asked, "Do you have *mujer* [woman]?" instead of *major* (meaning "better").

These problematic situations are historically rooted. Nearly five centuries ago, arriving Spanish and Portuguese colonizers established large private estates (*latifundios*) on which the indigenous rural population (Indios and Guarani in Paraguay) as well as imported African workers were employed for inferior agricultural labor in cattle raising and the production of sugarcane, tobacco, coffee, and timber for export. The Spanish and Portuguese landlords considered the farmworkers (*campesinos*) a legitimate part of their land-tenure rights. The campesinos' conditions worsened over time until the Mexican revolution of 1911 introduced new land-tenure concepts. *Latifundia* was abolished and conditional private ownership was established, accountable to restrictions designed to serve the public interest, such as setting a maximum land-ownership size and protecting the interests of the peasants cultivating the land. The distributive land-reform measures of Mexico were later implemented in Bolivia in 1952–59 and in Cuba in 1959.

In Paraguay, despite the wide use of the term *land reform* (*reforma agraria*), it was politically misused, referring to two different policies. One was the settlement of state-owned land and cleared forest areas, without government intervention in the existing distribution of large landholdings. The second was conceived primarily in juridical terms, limiting the program to defining the legal status of the settler and his or her rights with respect to the land without considering the related institutional factors in agricultural production, such as secure access to credit, access to improved seeds, and marketing services. This latter program did not consider the welfare aspects of land distribution—that is, the households' distribution of income and consumption at the community and national levels. This narrow legal conception was manifested in the academic qualification of senior staff and project managers, who were graduates of the law college. Both the Paraguayan minister of agriculture and the president of the Agrarian Reform Institute, with whom I was directly working, belonged to this legal-qualification category. In addition, the minister was the secretary-general of the ruling party (*Colorado*) representing the interests of the large colonization schemes and the commercially oriented large farming units that were dominated by those who migrated from Germany, Italy, and Russia during and after the Second World War. In fact, the president of Paraguay himself was of German origin.

Furthermore, most of the staff of the agrarian-reform department was stationed at its headquarters in Asuncion, leaving the countryside offices largely to clerks without technical staff. Another deficiency was the lack of reliable data on landholding and ownership sizes, as there was serious doubt about the results of the recently conducted 1950 agricultural census. This problem was compounded by considering land-rights data to be of a military nature, and accordingly the Cadastral Survey Agency belonged to the army and the Ministry of Defense, which was difficult to access.

Given these realities and under these circumstances, what could an FAO/UN land-reform expert do?

I began with the organization of a national seminar, chaired by the minister of agriculture himself with participation of department heads, the presidents of the Agricultural Credit Bank, the Agrarian Reform Institute (ARI), the Cadastral Survey Agency, the University of Asuncion, the chief of the Agricultural Cooperatives Organization, and heads of nongovernmental organizations assisting the indigenous people as well as the representatives of land settlers. The purpose was to create an understanding of the multidisciplinary meaning of agrarian reform as a component of development economics. It was intended to achieve the rural-welfare objectives in Paraguay beyond its narrow legal connotation.

The seminar was widely reported in the press and broadcast in its entirety by the national radio. It was followed first in 1958 by a three-week training course for the ARI's technical staff. My lectures given at the training course were published jointly (in Spanish) by the FAO and the government of Paraguay under the title *Economia de la Tierra* (1959).

Secondly, the follow-up action included the reorganization of the structure of ARI to have an interdisciplinary board of directors, representing all government agencies that participated in the national seminar.

Thirdly, the government agreed to my proposal to change the title of the institute to the Institute of Rural Welfare (*Instituto de Bienestar Rural*).

The fourth follow-up action to the seminar was my proposed draft law for the settlement of unauthorized landless occupants whom I studied and who illegally occupied the abandoned but fertile state-owned land. According to the plan, they would become new owners, having property title to their land in the Eastern Province on the border with Brazil and along the Parana River. In that plan, all technical and institutional factors examined during the national seminar were provided, and the new settlers were interviewed and selected by those who completed their in-service training indicated earlier.

My field service in Latin America took an interesting turn in 1958 and 1959, when I assisted the governments of Cuba and Bolivia in the implementation of the distributive land reforms. Such redistribution introduced radical changes in the development of the economies and the structure of the social systems in both countries.

Cuba

My Cuban field experience began in August 1959, three months after the proclamation of the land-reform law and in response to a written request to the FAO/UN from Mr. Antonio Jimenez, head of the Agrarian Reform Institute, and Dr. Regino Boti, the minister of economic affairs of Cuba. I was fortunate to have a meeting with President Fidel Castro, who succinctly explained the reform objectives: sharply reducing gross inequality, abolishing tenancy and "all forms of exploitation," diversifying and intensifying agricultural production within a centrally planned system, and "liberating" sharecroppers and landless workers from the monopolistic powers of large absentee landowners and the Americans who dominated the cattle and sugar plantations. Briefly, the prereform gross inequality was manifested in the fact that only 9 percent of the total number of landowners held 73 percent of Cuba's total arable land. A few American landowners controlled 52 percent of the total production of sugar and meat, on which the economy depended.

In the process of redistributing expropriated privately landed properties, I proposed lowering the size of the already-proclaimed beneficiaries' units (of thirty hectares each) both to expand the scale of the reform beneficiaries and meet the desired income level of the households. It was decided, later in 1963, to reduce the size of the distributed units from thirty to sixteen hectares and to expropriate an additional area of 25 percent of privately owned farms over the size of sixty-seven hectares, each for their direct management by the state people's farms, which gradually grew in area and number to reach 83 percent of the total arable land. In the meantime, the other productive asset (education combined with health service) was provided to all Cubans, free of charge. Consequently, by 1986 illiteracy and absolute poverty had been almost eradicated by way of the massive redistribution of productive assets such as land, education, and capital. In spite of unfavorable conditions, like the drought in 1961, followed by the hurricane of 1963, and the emigration of many technical staff to the United States, growth in sugar and maize production was sustained, and irrigated areas were expanded.

Bolivia

My fieldwork in Bolivia during 1958 and 1959 was arranged after the traditional economy and social structure were transformed by the 1952 revolution, which abolished latifundia (large private farms and plantations combined with land monopoly) and redistributed land-property rights in favor of the indigenous people (native *Indios* speaking *Quechua*) and their emancipation from the powerful Spanish landowners who encroached upon the indigenous people's communal land in the Altiplano (altitude of about four thousand meters), as well as in subtropical zones of the Yungas and the Oriente. My case study of the 3,600-hectare Taraco communal area of the Indios near Lake Titicaca illustrates the extent of social injustice, the abolition of which was a major objective of the land reform. This realignment of property did not fix a single maximum limit on land, owing to the wide variation in climatic and agronomic conditions.

In brief, the results of my assessment of the Bolivian reform policies may be summarized as follows:

1. The reform measures had significantly reduced the extreme inequality and injustice among the 72 percent of the total population who were engaged in agricultural activities. Yet less attention was given to production, considering that the beneficiaries were mostly living in communal villages, having religious and social values with little knowledge of production practices of crops and grazing. The reform preserved the system of communal tenure of land, and it was oriented by way of a joint cooperative production organization and provided modern agricultural techniques through credit-cum-technical guidance, cadastral surveying, and title registration. I pointed out the need for applying the same approach of integrated services in the new land-settlement areas and the specification of clear land-title records.

2. The developmental consequences of deficient statistical information was stressed to government officials, particularly those

resulting from the absence of data on land titles, tenancies, farm wages, and household income and consumption.

3. The professional training of the staff engaged in the implementation and study of rural-development programs was inadequate. Generally, they were either lawyers or agricultural engineers without the necessary economic and social-science orientation. Clearly, the legal staff was needed, but only in a specific area of development. Their university training was lacking in systematic knowledge of the principles of economics, sociology, anthropology, and political science related to understanding rural development. In my seminars given to both the technical and administrative staff, I explained the interrelated concepts in understanding the difference between agricultural growth and economic development, emphasizing the importance not merely of total production but also and importantly its equitable distribution to realize the welfare gains to the rural poor.

Brazil

A halfhearted land-reform law was issued in 1964 whose implementation suffered from conflicting interests demonstrated through the political power structure, primarily with regard to the interpretation of land expropriation "for the public interest." Hence, by 1984, the Brazilian reform was limited to pilot land-development/settlement schemes in the northeastern region, where only 1 percent of the total area proclaimed by the government for redistribution to poor peasants was actually implemented. In the meantime, land concentration substantially increased, and the absolute poverty level in rural areas increased, reaching 50 percent of the total rural population in 1980 and rising to 61 percent in 1988. Also, 60 percent of the Brazilian total arable land in 1984 was owned by only 5 percent of the total landholders, enjoying generous agricultural credit subsidies and tax incentives. Kay (1988) attributes increasing poverty to land concentration and to the rising numbers of landless workers.

This distributional inequality was a feature of the long-established and complex Brazilian system of dominant capitalism both in the urban industrial areas and in the rural sectors. In the latter, coffee plantations and feudalism prevailed. In the meantime, the demand for social reforms increased among the workers' trade unions and in the Amazon and other poor peasant areas. This capitalist system prevailed without redistributive land reform and without changing the bias toward coffee plantations and against food crops in areas where poverty and surplus labor existed. The ideology has been based on the belief that with urban industrial growth, poverty would be gradually and slowly alleviated—a form of "trickle-down" economics.

Since the 1970s, the strength of the socialist workers' unions in rural areas has succeeded in giving priority to the reform of the land-tenure system and to poverty reduction. Accordingly, the landless, the land occupants having no title to the land, and the indigenous rural people, supported by the trade unions of urban workers, have increased their demands for land and social security (Leite 1994).

Ecuador

In 1984, I was invited by the country's vice president in charge of the newly established Integrated Rural Development (IRD) program to assess its progress and advise on improving its field activities. The program consisted of a wide range of activities, including land settlement of an indigenous population totaling seven hundred thousand people. Out of the total seventeen planned projects, only seven were functioning, with families settled on public, uncultivated land.

I quickly discovered a program in almost total disarray. The new settlers were unable to benefit from the established stores of subsidized consumer products. Moreover, credit supplied by the Ecuador Central Bank was not supported by either the Peasant Development Department or the

National Peasant Training Institute of the Ministry of Agriculture. These different entities functioned separately, without cooperation or a clear purpose. In addition, I noted that the peasants were organized in their traditional communes as part of the national political system. The government had created a People's Advancement Program to reinforce the peasants' participation. I also found that, in the process of social development (education, employment, and participation in decision making), women were excluded from *cabildos*, the community town centers in the Sierra.

C. African Countries

The variation in the classification of countries by international organizations presents an analytical problem. For example, whereas some organizations classify Libya, Tunisia, Sudan, and Morocco as Middle Eastern, others include them in the African region. I experienced this problem during my work with the FAO and also in addressing development issues in my books and seminars. Within the UN system, the FAO considers Morocco, Algeria, Tunisia, Sudan, and Libya as Middle Eastern countries served by the regional office in Cairo, although they officially belong to the program of work of the United Nations Economic Commission for Africa (UNECA), with its headquarters in Addis Ababa, Ethiopia. Another difficulty arises from dividing African development issues in North Africa, Francophone sub-Saharan Africa, and Africa south of the Sahara. I have addressed the development implications of this confusing situation in *Land, Food and Rural Development in North Africa* (1993).

Evaluating the Work of the African Centre for Rural Development

This was my second major fieldwork in Africa in 1992, funded by the FAO in response to the recommendation of the governing council of the Centre on Integrated Rural Development in Africa. The center was established in Arusha, Tanzania, in 1983, to meet the needs expressed by people from sixteen African governments at their conference of 1979. At that time, they committed themselves to contributing annually to its budget to supplement the financial assistance granted by the United Nations. My main task was to lead a three-person mission of experts from Tanzania, Kenya, and Malawi, with a focus on judging the work of the center against the needs of its sixteen African founders.

Accordingly, I visited eight countries (Tanzania, Uganda, Ethiopia, Kenya, Malawi, Somalia, Sudan, and Ghana) and held discussions with FAO officials in Rome and Accra as well as the senior staff of the UN Economic Commission for Africa in Addis Ababa.

I investigated this post-1980 policy issue because of an obvious contradiction: despite strong arguments for maintaining customary land tenure, including arguments by the World Bank itself, and in spite of a lack of hard evidence on the production superiority of private/freehold/individual tenure over communally owned customary landownership, a privatization policy under the World Bank's and Western countries' neoliberal reforms was instituted and vigorously pursued in many African countries. Moreover, privatization of landownership was enforced *in spite of* empirical evidence that the secure and inheritable customary tenure system is as compatible with the production of export crops as with food production. It is also compatible in production incentives and risk reduction (as documented in Feder and Noronha 1987 as well as in Feder and Nishio 1998). The experience of African countries is briefly presented with a detailed explanation of Uganda and Ethiopia.

Uganda

Based on a carefully conducted empirical analysis of a sampled survey of private (*malio*) land versus customary landholdings in Uganda by Gombya-Ssembajjwe et al. (2001) and Place and Otsuka et al. (2001), the findings show that customary land tenure has, for a long time, enjoyed statutory protection. The results of their study suggest also that there are no differences in investment incentives between the two systems in coffee planting. Nevertheless, the Land Act of 1998 in Uganda stipulates the conversion of customary land into private (freehold) land property at a time when a large number of wealthy farmers held "leased" customary land.

Besides Uganda, all available studies on land-tenure systems in Kenya, Malawi, Sudan, and South Africa agree that land has, for centuries, been communally owned by indigenous groups (tribes, families, and communities). The groups devised sets of working rules for land rights (use and occupancy) and subsisted by grazing and cultivating food crops when rain permitted. As recognized by anthropologists and geographers, this customary land tenure has been not only the most suitable socioecological system for land use and livestock husbandry in semiarid agriculture, but also the cornerstone of food security and social security for millions of indigenous people. Likewise, its contribution to economic growth includes

1. employment of the pastoralists' family members within a rational division of labor of women and children; and
2. the production of a considerable part of the countries' total meat, milk, wool, and hides, necessary for a minimum standard of living.

It is difficult to understand why non-African professionals still see this customary system as backward or primitive and in need of being privatized according to the conventional Anglo-Saxon conception of efficiency in agricultural production by way of individual private ownership of land linked to the capital market. Despite strong arguments for maintaining customary land tenure, and in spite of a lack of empirical evidence on the production superiority of individual private landownership over customary tenure arrangements, privatization policies are pursued with vigor in most African countries. They are also enforced in spite of widely available empirical evidence that customary tenure is compatible both with the production of export crops and with food production. The experience of several privatizing countries suggests the following:

1. The vulnerability of individual owners to the loss of land to urban speculators as well as to mortgage and heavy indebtedness.
2. The weakening of women's customary rights in land and command over food.
3. The shift away from food crops toward cash/export crops.
4. Because of high transaction costs, the land buyers are mostly businesspeople, politicians, senior civil servants, members of the armed forces, and larger landowners.

Table 1: A Quantitative Profile of Selected Rural Development Issues in Sixteen African Countries, 1970s–1990s

Country	Incidence of Rural Poverty				Food Insecurity						Arable Land per Head of Agric. Population % Change During	Adult Illiteracy Total % (Aged 15+)
	% of Rural Population		Number (million)		% Dependency on Food Imports		Per Person Food Production Average Annual Change %		Agric. Labor Productivity Average Annual Change %			
	1977–79	1988	1977–79	1988–90	1971	1988–90	1979–81	1981–89	1971–80	1981–89	1975–1991	1990
	(1)				(2)		(3)		(4)		(5)	(6)
Benin	65	65	1.6	1.8	6	12	0.6	3.3	2.2	6.1	-11	77
Congo	n.a.	80	n.a.	0.9	13	25	-0.7	-0.9	0.2	0.6	-20	43
Egypt	25	25	5.3	6.7	20	43	-0.8	1.0	0.5	1.4	-20	52
Kenya	50	55	6.5	9.9	7	10	-1.6	1.2	0.3	1.9	-35	31
Lesotho	55	n.a.	0.7	n.a.	30	50	-1.0	-1.2	-0.9	0.3	-31	n.a.
Malawi	85	90	3.5	6.1	4	6	-0.9	-2.5	1.4	-0.2	-11	n.a.
Mozambique	n.a.	65	n.a.	7.4	7	22	-3.1	-2.1	-3.4	-0.9	-30	67
Nigeria	38	51	25.0	35.8	3	4	-2.0	1.9	-1.1	3.3	-32	49

Senegal	n.a.	70	n.a.	3.1	31	38	-2.9	0.1	-2.5	0.9	-35	38
Sierra Leone	65	65	1.7	1.8	15	19	-0.5	-2.4	1.1	-0.3	-8	79
Sudan	70	85	9.9	15.9	9	15	0.4	-3.1	0.5	-1.4	-17	73
Tanzania	60	60	9.0	11.9	5	3	1.7	-1.1	2.2	0.3	-35	n.a.
Togo	n.a.	30	n.a.	0.7	5	21	-1.5	0.4	-0.6	2.2	-33	57
Uganda	n.a.	80	12.4	n.a.	2	1	-2.1	-3.0	-2.0	-1.5	-42	52
Zaire	80	80	12.9	16.6	5	5	-1.1	-0.9	1.2	0.5	-32	28
Zambia	52	80	0.8	2.9	22	7	-0.2	1.4	1.2	2.3	n.a.	27

Notes: n.a. = not available. Incidence of rural poverty is the estimated percentage and numbers of rural population living in absolute poverty (i.e., falling below the poverty line established by each country). Dependency on food imports is the percentage of food imports (including food aid) to total domestic food supply for consumption. Agricultural labor productivity is output per head of the working force in agriculture, calculated from FAO, Country Tables—1991.

Sources: Column (1) IFAD, "The State of World Rural Poverty," 1992, Table 6, and El-Ghonemy, "The Political Economy of Rural Poverty," London: Routledge 1990, Appendix A. Column (2) UNDP, "Human Development Report," 1993, Table 3. Column (3) FAO, "Country Tables—1991." Column (4) See notes above. Column (5) calculated from FAO "Country Tables—1991." Column (6) World Bank, "World Development Report 1992," Table 1 of Indicators.

These nonagricultural land speculators know the law and registration procedures, and they have contacts with credit institutions and land surveyors. Financially, they can afford the costs of surveying, registration, and issuing private title deeds.

The primary effect of privatization on rural well-being is increasing insecurity, in terms of both the loss of household command over food and the loss of customary rights to land. In Malawi, between 1986 and 1990, the area of customary land that was privatized doubled. Land buyers converted the production of food crops into burley tobacco, and former small landholders became wageworkers and net buyers of food. With the population growing fast, at 3.7 percent per year, food production per person fell rapidly (see table 1). In contrast, tobacco production increased from 70,000 tons in 1986 to 110,000 tons in 1991. In Uganda, the economic policy reform toward export-led growth has facilitated shifting land use from grazing and growing food (cassava and millet) to commercial ranching managed by urban land buyers who have kinship relations with influential policy makers, as documented in two districts in Malawi. The buyers erected fences around their ranches, depriving pastoral households in the surrounding areas of traditional corridors used for their own passage and the grazing of their animals.

No matter how good the neoclassical economic principles of privatization, the loss of households' command over their food needs, coupled with falling food productivity and after-market orientation, should be of serious concern to governments, international organizations, and development analysts. FAO data show a post-1980 downward trend in food production per person in sub-Saharan Africa compared with other regions: the index for 1990–94 is below the average for 1979–81, and the rates of growth in average daily calorie intake per person have also declined in most countries. These data are worrying indeed with regard to the food insecurity of rural households and their increasing dependence on the imperfect market for food acquisition and the increasing incidence of chronic undernutrition, particularly among young children.

Ethiopia

During my field study in 1983, I realized that Ethiopia had never had a population census taken before my visit. I relied, therefore, on several estimates made in 1980 showing that the total population was thirty million, mostly inhabiting the highlands. Therein 14 percent were urban and 86 percent were rural, according to the ambiguous criteria used. The agricultural population was also estimated at 66 percent of the total labor force.

The dearth of data limited my examination of the progress made in rural development, particularly the absence of disaggregated data by residence into rural and urban, as well as by occupation and sex. What was certainly serious in my development-economics field study was the *absence* of facts on the distribution of wealth and the socioeconomic characteristics of the population before and after the 1974 revolutionary change that was introduced by the military. This analytical difficulty was compounded by the revolution's introduction of changes in 1974 of the names of the country's districts. Important was the enactment of a radical land reform on socialist principles in 1975 according to which

1. all cultivated lands were made the collective property of the state;
2. the farmers were organized in peasant associations to manage their secured rights in land tenure after tenancy arrangements were abolished; and
3. there was agreement of the state farms (whose area represented 5 percent of the total cultivated land) to become the direct responsibility of government officials.

In my attempt to estimate the incidence of rural poverty, I found its nearest indicator was undernutrition, which, according to estimates made by the Ethiopian Nutrition Institute, reached 20 percent among the total population and 40 percent of the total number of children.

In addition, 60 percent of the children were *underweight* with poor health because of drinking unpurified water directly from the river or lakes. Available information for characterizing poverty suggested that in 1974, nearly 90 percent of the adult rural population was illiterate. Accordingly the revolutionary government introduced the National Literacy Campaign, in which the peasant associations were active; this campaign was successful in reducing illiteracy to nearly 77 percent, according to the results of surveys conducted in the districts of Sbewa and Bale.

In a subsequent visit to Ethiopia's rural areas, I learned that this notable progress was achieved despite the use of nearly fifteen local languages. Also, I found that agriculture continued to be the backbone of the economy, with coffee exports bringing 65 percent of the total foreign exchange—used mostly for the purchase of arms and grain imports. But in my conversations with local villagers, I heard several complaints about deficient grain supply and high consumer prices despite the land reform's provision of tenure security to all landholders. I learned also that credit supply was "adequate," as the priority in its allocation was given to state farms, which received 85 percent of the total agricultural credit supply, together with the coffee producers.

North Africa

In my 1993 North Africa study, I focused on three development issues:

1. The importance of historical events, particularly the foreign occupation, in shaping the countries' socioeconomic conditions.
2. The impact of the vigorous revival of Islamic fundamentalism on distributive fairness.
3. The changing roles of both the market and the state in the distribution of property rights and in alleviating rural poverty. A special effort was made to find out whether the size distribution of land and income was determined by a combination of historical and climatic conditions or by the Islamic principles of inheritance.

Historically, from the sixteenth century to the period 1920–50, North Africa was ruled by European countries, the longest colonial rule being in Algeria starting with the Ottoman Turks, followed by the French and Italians in the Maghreb and the British in Egypt. These European colonizers shared a common interest: extracting exorbitant land taxes from the fellaheen through assigned local agents in exchange for large landholdings and sociopolitical powers. While the French colonizers produced wine from growing grapes—against Islamic principles that prohibit drinking alcohol—the British expanded cotton production and its export to Britain's textile industry. Nevertheless, the colonizers introduced market economy and technology, including modern irrigation methods.

Understanding Farm-Size Fragmentation in Egypt and Morocco

Economists studying land use in North Africa have expressed concern over the efficiency of the size of landholdings and its successive fragmentation. I examined the situation in both Egypt and Morocco, particularly in regard to inheritance arrangements. To focus on this issue, we must distinguish between *fragmentation* and *subdivision* of land. The former denotes the altered feature of subdivision of land, by which the divided parcels of a single holding are separated by different distances. *Subdivision*, on the other hand, is the process of dividing up a single landholding into several farming units, usually through sale and inheritance arrangements.

In my field study of Morocco, I showed that an area of one parcel was one-tenth of the average area of the total holdings. However, the use of *average* conceals the extent and distribution of fragmented holdings, as well as variation by locality. For example, in the Moroccan district of Taounate, 68 percent of the total holdings in the village of Kari aba-Mohammad were below 10 hectares each and were fragmented into twelve tiny plots on average, each about 9.7 hectares, whereas the average number of plots in each holding at the level of the entire agricultural sector was seven plots or parcels.

In Egypt, the results of the 1982 agricultural census showed that 65 percent of the total landholdings were fragmented into more than four parcels each. Moreover, the size of some parcels was so minute that on average, each parcel was about one-tenth of a hectare, although the national average was almost one complete hectare.

At this point of discussion, two questions are raised:

1. Does the prevalence of small holdings constrain productivity?
2. Are the Islamic principles of inheritance to blame for the continuous fragmentation of landholdings in Middle Eastern agriculture?

To answer the first question, I collected the data given in table 2 on the extent of small holdings as defined by each country and the average number of parcels in each holding.

Table 2. The Extent of Small Landholdings and Their Fragmentation in Algeria, Egypt, Libya, Morocco, and Tunisia, 1950–82

| Country | Year | Average Size of | | Average Number of | |
		% of Total Number	All Sizes in Hectares	Holdings Hectares	Parcels per Holding in All Size Classes
Algeria	1973	50.1	1.7	6.2	n.a.
Egypt	1950	78.5	0.7	2.3	2.5
	1961	84.0	0.6	1.6	2.7
	1982	90.0	0.6	1.1	2.2
Libya	1974	n.a.	n.a.	13.0	3.4
Morocco	1974	74.0	1.6	4.9	7.0
	1962	70.0	2.0	5.1	n.a.
Tunisia	1961	41.0	2.3	15.4	4.2
	1980	44.0	2.2	14.4	n.a

Notes: For Algeria, Morocco, and Tunisia, a "small holding" is less than five hectares. For Egypt it is less than two hectares. *Number of parcels per holding* refers to holdings that have more than one parcel.

Sources: Results of the censuses of agriculture, except Tunisia, 1980, which is from *Enquête Agricole de Base* and the National Institute of Statistics, Tunis.

The Extent of Small Holdings

Table 2 shows that the percentage of small holdings is high, particularly in Egypt and Morocco, implying the influence of population pressure on scarce agricultural land. However, the data should be considered country specific and therefore does not permit perfect intercountry comparisons for three reasons. The first is the variation in land productivity—that is, whether the land is irrigated or rain fed, fertile or infertile, and so on. The second is the difference among countries in their use of the concept of holding: whereas Algeria included only private holdings in the census, others covered all holdings (private, cooperative, and state farms). The third reason is that the size of small holdings is arbitrarily established as a cutoff point and is, therefore, disputable. Given these limitations, table 2 suggests two tendencies.

The first is an increasing percentage of small farms in Egypt and Tunisia, combined with a decline in their average area, which implies a relative increase in the proportion of poor landholders. The opposite direction of change in Morocco is perhaps caused by the accelerated implementation of the land-consolidation program in *perimetres d'irrigation* in the second half of the 1970s. The other tendency is the high ratio between the average area per holding at the aggregate level and that of small holdings, ranging from seven times as much in Tunisia to less than twice in Egypt.

But as I asked earlier, does the prevalence of small-sized farms bring about adverse production effects? In principle, it should not. Empirical evidence indicates that small farms intensify the use of both land and family labor. The results of the 1982 agricultural census in Egypt and Morocco point out that small holdings have a much higher degree of land-use and cropping intensity than large holdings, as indicated below by size in percentage.

Table 3. Cropped Area per Holding in Egypt and Morocco, 1982

	Egypt		Morocco	
	Under 2 Ha.	Over 20 Ha.	Under 5 Ha.	Over 20 Ha.
Cropped Area per Holding	99.2%	55–75%	79%	2–8%

Another indicator is output per unit of land by size of farm. In irrigated areas, crop yields and gross value of output per hectare were higher in small farms compared with larger ones of Algeria, Morocco, and Tunisia, according to the findings of a World Bank study. The study reports, "There is evidence in all three countries that small farmers in irrigated areas are more efficient than larger hectares" (see Cleaver 1982, 50).

The Influence of Islamic Principles of Inheritance on Land Fragmentation

In my seminars and in my book on North Africa (1993), I addressed the second question about the effects of Islamic principles of inheritance on the fragmentation of holdings from one generation to the next.

As I understood them, these Islamic principles (*mirath*) aim to preserve a person's property or estate within his or her family and guarantee the rights of legitimate inheritors and creditors after death (*fouroud al-tarikah*), to be subdivided in clearly stipulated shares (*naseeb*) after meeting the funeral expenses and the debts owed to creditors. These arrangements are laid down in precise terms in the Quran's al-Nisaa and al-Baqarah chapters (on these principles, see Abu-Zahra 1963, 25). The principles also included arrangements for avoiding subdivision (*takharog*) by which an heir may withdraw in favor of one or all the remaining inheritor-heirs, against compensation to be volitionally agreed upon by the parties concerned.

This means that the physical splitting of inherited agricultural land is not mandatory. Rather, it can be retained and managed as a single production unit on behalf of the heirs by one of them whom they trust and who is experienced in farming. Islamic financial institutions can also lend the heir the amount of the required compensation. Hence, the principles are neither to be solely blamed for the continued subdivision of landholdings (farm size), nor are they to blame for the inability of governments to enforce existing laws, setting limits below which an ownership cannot be divided and registered.

There are also such noninheritance factors as

1. population pressure on scarce land;
2. the increasing demand for leasing or purchasing land belonging to absentee landowners;
3. remittances of migrant workers that encourage small landowners to sell parcels at inflated prices; and
4. the impact of rapid urbanization on the demand for converting agricultural land for nonagricultural purposes.

Hence, the noninheritance factors operating in the dynamic national economy contribute in varying degrees to the extent of subdivision and fragmentation of agricultural land.

D. Asian Countries

Earlier, I pointed out the different grouping of countries into geographical regions practiced by several international agencies, according to which Afghanistan and Pakistan belong to the Middle/Near East and not to the Asian region, which in turn is classified into Far East, Southeast Asia, and so on. Keeping this variation in mind, I present, in this section, my field experience in the following countries: India, Nepal, the Philippines, Indonesia, Sri Lanka, and Bangladesh.

India

Based on the long experience of India in tackling such problems of rural underdevelopment as land concentration and poverty, I focus here on examining government efforts during my three field visits to India in the 1950s and 1970s. During the earlier visits, my concern was about understanding why the fervor in advancing land reform since the early 1950s had floundered. My interviews with senior officials in the Planning Commission, the Revenue Department of West Bengal, and several scholars at academic institutions have revealed the wide gap between idealism on the one hand and constraining inadequacies in implementation capabilities on the other (such as the actual performance of cooperatives, the corruption in local government bureaucracy that was in charge of field implementation, and so on). For example, I learned how some landlords gained back their land from tenants who were the beneficiaries from land reform. However, the result was manifested in the fact that *only 3 percent* of India's total privately owned land was actually redistributed. Also, the ineffective implementation resulted in the fact that the degree of landholding concentration, in terms of the Gini index, remained high at 0.621. The Gini index (developed by the Italian sociologist Corrado Gini) is a measure of statistical dispersion intended to represent the income distribution of a nation's residents and is the most commonly used measure of inequality. During my subsequent visits and because of India's extensive geographical scope and interstate variation, I concentrated my attention on the state of Kerala, where land reform was effectively implemented (18 percent of private land was redistributed, and tenancy was abolished). Accordingly, while the incidence of rural poverty was reduced in all of India from 54.1 percent in 1957 to 46.1 percent in 1974, it was reduced to a lower level in the state of Kerala, from 50.3 to 40.9 percent (see table 4). In this regard, the influence of the socialist labor trade union in Kerala must be mentioned.

Table 4. Variation in Poverty Reduction in All India and the State of Kerala, 1956–78

		Incidence of Poverty	
		Rural Poor %	**No. Rural Poor (In Millions)**
All India	1956–57	54.1	178.5
	1973–74	46.1	208.4
State of Kerala	1961–62	50.3	7.1
	1977–78	40.9	7.4

Source: Montek S. Ahluwalia, "Rural Poverty, Agricultural Production and Prices: A Re-examination," in Mellow and Desai (eds.), *Agricultural Change and Rural Poverty*, 1985.

Turning now to what had happened to India's commitment for land-reform policy since the early 1950s, my investigation revealed that throughout, the fundamental principles laid down in 1947 by the Congress Party Committee on Agrarian Reform were maintained. Private property rights in land and other means of production were adopted within a socially complex class system and in different states, some of which have populations exceeding eighty million. Constitutionally, each state makes independent decisions about its land-reform policy and implementation. Between 1952 and 1974, virtually all states enacted numerous laws that

1. fixed ceilings on private landownership;
2. abolished intermediaries in tenancy arrangements; and
3. controlled rental values and fixed minimum wage rates in agriculture.

As progressive as all this may seem, these pieces of regulatory legislation were designed with such deliberate exemptions and legal loopholes that they could not meet the rising expectations of the mass of rural poor. By 1974, *only 3 percent of the privately owned land in India had been redistributed.*

With regard to the broader policy issues of antipoverty rural development, I found out that India's rural-development program since the early 1960s included

1. community-development programs under which one hundred villages with sixty-five thousand people total were to constitute an administrative block with service cooperatives established in each village;
2. an intensive area-development program that concentrated mostly on irrigated areas with a technological thrust for increasing the yields of wheat using tractors and tube wells (as a result, the wheat-growing areas in northern India benefitted most from this program);
3. credit-supply programs for small and marginal farmers;
4. the rapid expansion in irrigated land during the 1970s; and
5. integrated rural-development programs and a national rural-employment program.

Among other national programs affecting the rural poor, a population-control policy was targeted to reduce the fertility rates in the large family groups who were mostly the poor.

Nepal

My visit was arranged by the government of Nepal, to focus on examining the development issues and related policy matters of immediate priority to the government with regard to its Five-Year Development Plan 1981–85.

Nepal lies north of India at the foot of the Himalayas. Unlike most of the countries I studied, Nepal had virtually none of the infrastructural facilities essential to initiating poverty-alleviation programs in rural areas. Despite the formulation of the first Five-Year Development Plan 1976–80, I found the economy lacking basic data on prices and wages. Even where government departments' data existed, their time-frame comparability was difficult, primarily because of frequent changes in the definitions they used. However, when the reliability of the data was found to be questionable, I indicated this defect to the authorities concerned. These data limitations are stressed here, since the primary purpose of my study was to assess the extent of rural poverty and to examine the changes related to agrarian reform and rural development.

In contrast to Nepal's scenic beauty and cultural pluralism stands the stark reality of poverty. I found that most of the population of fifteen million in 1981 lived at subsistence level and were illiterate, undernourished, and lacking in basic medical care. Nearly 90 percent of its total population in 1981 depended on agriculture, and about 95 percent lived in rural areas. Agriculture generated nearly two-thirds of the national income and 85 percent of the total export earnings. Almost 65 percent of the farming population consisted of small subsistence farmers, mostly tenants working plots of less than three acres each. The landless wage-dependent agricultural workers represented about 90 percent of the total labor force in 1981.

But only 17 percent of the total land was under cultivation, mostly in the hills, where the average holding was less than one acre each. With a stagnant agriculture and the population growing annually at 2.5 percent, the real per capita income of the agricultural population must have declined over the 1970s, and according to my study, the average income in urban areas in 1980 was eleven times that in the rural areas.

Technological advances in the post-1975 period (improved seeds and the use of chemical fertilizers) benefitted the larger landholders most, whereas the small farmers and the landless workers received little or no benefit. The same pattern occurred with the distribution of benefits from the generous foreign aid, which contributed 58 percent of the total public expenditures and 22 percent of the public investment in agriculture.

To emphasize this point, the presentation of the 1977 data from the agricultural Credit Bank and the results of the ILO study (1982) are helpful. These studies showed that 64 percent of the total landholdings were less than two acres each and represented 11 percent of the total cultivated area in 1982. By contrast, those in the group holding (owning/renting) forty acres or more made up only 1 percent of the total landholders, yet their land area was 21 percent of the cultivated land.

From my field investigation and interviews in the Ministry of Land Reform and the Ministry of Finance, as well as in the National Planning Commission and the Central Bureau of Statistics, it was clear that His Majesty's Government of Nepal was concerned about the worsening conditions of most of the rural population and accordingly issued two land-reform laws, establishing a ceiling on both landownership and tenancy. Also, subtenancy was abolished. As the reader would expect in such a messy institutional situation, the two laws remained a political show and were not effectively implemented. This fact was revealed by the careful study of the International Labour Organization in 1982, as well as an analytical study conducted by Mahesh C. Regmi of the University of California–Berkeley (1976). A verdict on the Nepalese government's outright failure was the available estimates of income distribution and poverty levels in rural areas made by the ILO "Employment and Basic Needs Field Survey" in 1982, as well as the FAO data on socioeconomic indicators for "Monitoring Agrarian Reform and Rural Development," prepared in 1983. The latter indicated that 42 percent of the total rural households were below the established minimum subsistence income or the poverty line, compared with an average of 22 percent in urban areas. Also, the FAO study on nutrition indicated that 38 percent of the total rural population suffered from undernutrition. Moreover, the 1971 population census showed that 96 percent of the rural women were illiterate compared with 75 percent of male adults.

In brief, my study concluded that the Nepalese government's strategy for achieving development solely through aggregate economic growth did *not* work and, though necessary, was not sufficient to realize real development in the absence of effective redistributive measures. Also, I pointed out to the government that the lack of political commitment and the incompetence of its bureaucracy constituted a single development problem.

The Philippines
I visited the Philippines twice, once in the 1980s and again in 1990, in my capacity as deputy director of the FAO Rural Development Division and as chairman of the FAO Committee for Monitoring Poverty Alleviation.

In March 1990, my hosts were the Department of Agrarian Reform, the NGO Coalition, and the University of the Philippines at Los Banos. In both visits, I found that land-reform policy issues were hotly debated, and my doubts increased about whether government programs were reaching the landless poor who were the intended beneficiaries. These programs included the Agricultural Tenancy Act, the Agricultural Land Reform Code, and land-settlement schemes in Mindanao and Banisian, where nearly 850,000 hectares were settled by former squatters on public land. They also established associations for the beneficiaries of land reform, called Samahang Nayon, and rural banks for agricultural credit supply, as well as the employment-generating program known as Kilusang Kibuhayan to help the landless workers, forestry workers, and poor fishermen.

Throughout my 1990 field study and my investigations at the Department of Land Reform and other organizations, my twin concerns were to judge the government's genuine commitment to reducing rural poverty and to assess the existing poverty levels. Despite its knowledge of the poverty conditions in rural areas reflected in its 1978–82 development plan, the government—in my view—was hiding behind the work of many foreign missions, including the World Bank and the FAO, with the anticipation of receiving their aid and recommendations. I read the draft 1983–87 plan and found that it, like earlier plans, did *not* intend to tackle the root causes of the land tenure–based power structure manifested in the composition of the parliament and in the pattern of investment in which multinational corporations had the leading role. I also assessed several estimates of rural poverty, which used different pricing systems for estimating household income and expenditure surveys and did not consider interregional variations. For the year 1975, there were three estimates of the rural poverty line as follows:

The World Bank	4,962 pesos
The Philippines Development Academy	8,668 pesos
The Government Wage Commission	6,900 pesos

I found also that the land-reform program proposed in the Presidential Executive Order on Land Reform in May 1987, like the earlier two laws of 1954 and 1963, did not criticize increasing landholding concentration, even though the landless workers in agriculture represented nearly 40 percent of the total agricultural households. The three land-reform attempts left the fundamental features of the power structure of landlords, multi-nationals, and moneylenders virtually intact. Available data suggested that average income per landless worker was two thousand pesos, which was less than half the minimum income (see the poverty line shown above) established by the World Bank for 1975. The share of the bottom 30 percent of the total rural population fell by 20 percent between 1970 and 1980, a period when the so-called land-reform laws were ineffective in adjusting rental rates for certain crops and not in all agricultural sectors.

Indonesia

I visited Indonesia together with Sri Lanka in 1985. The purpose of my visit was to explore the causal process of rural poverty with a special reference to the impact of the two world economic recessions in 1974–75 and 1980–83 on the two countries' rural-development programs. The early 1970s saw major economic changes: sharp increases in oil prices in 1973 and 1979, combined with a sharp rise in interest rates; and a decline in the rate of growth in the United States and Europe, leading to their falling demand for agricultural products of developing countries. Accordingly, manufactured exports from the United States and Europe fell by 12 percent in 1981 and 18 percent in 1982, the total foreign debts of developing countries increased sharply, and their real per capita income and rural living conditions deteriorated.

Indonesia's agricultural economy is huge (31 percent share of the gross domestic product compared with 18 percent from oil in 1980, in addition to having 65 percent of the total population of 125 million engaged in agriculture). I was surprised to find that the agricultural censuses of 1963 and 1973 did not include data on land tenure and the landless agricultural workers in the total 68,000 villages spread among 930 inhabited islands along the equator (of which I visited Java and Bali). I noted also that the 1973 agricultural census did not disaggregate the total population into urban and rural and that the census was based on a 5 percent sample data of the total 12.5 million agricultural population. In Java, the average farm size was half a hectare (nearly one acre) cultivated with rice and economically controlled by multinational corporations. The Central Office of Statistics told me that landless farmers, including tenants, were those holding less than 0.2 acres and that they represented 15 percent of the total agricultural households.

The government's concern over poverty was exhibited in the second Five-Year Development Plan (1974–78), which considered the 1960 Basic Agrarian Law as the foundation of property rights, and established in 1979 the large Land Settlement Scheme for which the National Commission on Agrarian Reform was set up. The purpose of the commission was to ensure the meeting of the plan's target of settling half a million households on land with five acres each, giving priority to "landless and near landless farmers" to cultivate the "Transmigration Land."

I recommended to the commission giving priority to land-title reg-istration to reduce the increasing land-tenure conflicts in rural areas and to ensure the settlers' access to agricultural credit and their benefit from the government's emphasis on high-yielding varieties of rice. To ensure the institutional participation of the settlers in production and in market-ing their produce, I suggested giving priority to the organization of the settlers' own cooperatives, free from the centrally planned economy and from the highly centralized government bureaucracy. The same was need-ed for the production and marketing of sugarcane, which was neglected after the independence of Indonesia in 1949. Small capital investment in labor-intensive industries in rural areas of Java were also recommended to compensate for the reduced employment opportunities that resulted from the rapid mechanization of agriculture and the effects of world recession, in terms of post-1976 falling per capita real income and real wages. Also, the annual rate of employment in agriculture fell from 0.7 percent in 1971 to 0.3 percent in 1980 in Java. Furthermore, real daily wages in agriculture in terms of kilograms of milled rice had been falling steadily in Java since

1975, according to the results of unpublished village studies carried out by B. White (1977 and 1979).

With regard to crude estimates of rural poverty, I considered that basic-needs costs in different localities could be useful in view of the extensive geographical area of sixty-eight thousand villages in 930 islands that make it difficult to establish a national poverty line.

Sri Lanka

In contrast to the giant area of Indonesia, this country is one small island inhabited by fifteen million, but its per capita income in 1983 was US$330 (nearly half that of Indonesia) and its life expectancy was much higher than Indonesia: seventy years and fifty-four years, respectively.

I visited Sri Lanka in 1985, two years after the outbreak of the civil war between the majority Hindu population and the minority Buddhist Tamils, who wanted their own separate state. My visit was part of my fieldwork for collecting material to edit *The Dynamics of Rural Poverty*, published in 1986 by FAO/UN, Rome. I found Sri Lanka well advanced both in socioeconomic studies on rural areas and in having a purposeful antipoverty program. According to the results of recently completed surveys, average per capita income in 1981 was 154 rupees in rural areas, compared with 238 rupees in urban areas. With regard to landholding distribution in 1982, I noted that 42.4 percent of the total number was less than one acre each; one to two acres were 21.9 percent, two to three acres were 13.6 percent, and between three and twenty acres were 22.1 percent.

I was impressed indeed by the width and depth of the country's rural-development program. The program, which received heavy foreign aid in the form of both grants and loans, included major irrigation works; the development of nearly seven hundred thousand acres for the settlement of landless and poor peasants; a public housing program; and a large, labor-intensive investment program, particularly for textile and clothing manufacture, which took advantage of cheap labor costs. In addition, the government promoted integrated rural-development schemes (IRDs) and implemented a land reform that was directed to areas not benefitting from large investment projects. I also visited the Kurengela district of irrigated rice and coconut crops cultivated by small farmers. The district pioneered rural-development schemes in 1979 with the assistance of the World Bank.

The implementation of IRD was begun by the Irrigation Department, which placed more emphasis on material physical aspects than on human and social aspects, particularly the effective participation of local small landholders. From interviewing many of them, I learned of their dissatisfaction with the design of the project coupled with the long delay in both the implementation and the price-subsidy support in the face of unstable prices and high inflation rates (14 percent annually in 1981–84). These issues increased the costs of production and eroded their profit margins from both rice and coconut crops. Also, I learned that the costs of the managerial staff were high because of considerable expenditure on purchasing an abundance of vehicles and other office services. Yet the staff have always reported success and given a rosy picture to the media, despite delays and serious production and marketing problems for the small farmers.

In the seminar I gave at the National Agrarian Research and Training Institute in Colombo, I presented my analytical remarks on the country's integrated rural development and the challenge of poverty alleviation. I praised the country's commitment to social justice in rural areas, manifested in such benefits as the government provision of free education and health service for all, rice subsidies, and the land-reform and major settlement programs. Accordingly, per capita income of the poorest 10 percent had increased in 1985 nearly four times since 1973–75. Through these agrarian redistributive programs, the government acquired nearly 63 percent of the total tea lands and 30 percent of the total rubber-cultivated land.

However, the results of consumer finances and socioeconomic surveys of 1979–82 suggest an increase in inequality of income distribution since the world recession of 1981–82, when the rich became richer and the poor stayed poor. Poverty estimates prepared jointly by the government and the FAO indicate that the rural residents who were absolutely poor represented 26 percent of the total rural population in 1981 (see El-Ghonemy, *The Dynamics of Rural Poverty*).

Bangladesh

Although I was living and working far away in Rome, I had close Bangladeshi ties. My boss in the FAO and a colleague working with me in a rural-poverty program were both Bangladeshi. I was also a friend of the director of the Bangladesh Institute of Development Studies in Dhaka. In 1983, the director kindly invited me for a discussion with him and the Land Reform Committee on the impact of the country's land-tenure system on rising poverty in rural areas, where nearly 90 percent of the total population lived.

To understand the country leadership's development objectives, I examined the draft Second Five-Year Development Plan for 1981–85, which stressed the objectives in generalized terms: raising the standard of living by way of supplying the basic needs, improvement of the quality of life in the rural areas through people participation, and to move towards an equitable distribution of income and opportunities for better social justice. The priorities were different from those of the earlier First Five-Year Plan of 1976, which specified economic growth as its major objective. Neither plan identified existing land-tenure arrangements as the main constraint in the development path. Nevertheless, I found that land reform was a subject of a heated debate and for which the Land Reform Committee (LRC) was established in 1982 under the chairmanship of the minister of agriculture.

I was able to obtain a copy of the LRC report, which recommended fixing a ceiling on cultivated land of nearly ten acres in "flood-free areas," which constitute a small proportion of the total cultivated land. Available data at the Dhaka Institute of Development Studies suggested that there would not be any significant surplus of land for redistribution, as only landholders owned ten acres and over. The expected benefits from the committee proposals were in the areas cultivating under the share-cropping arrangements, but under complicated bureaucratic provisions. I pointed out to members of the Land Reform Committee that the real target groups should have been the landless agricultural households who were growing in number at 5 percent annually and would be even higher if we added the "near-landless" category of ownership of less than one acre. The category of less than one acre in 1978 represented nearly 30 percent of the total rural households (about five million households), but their land area was only 8 percent of the total landownership area.

I visited the agricultural credit bank, established in 1979 for serving the small farmers in five out of twenty-one districts with financial assistance from the International Fund for Agricultural Development of the UN. Before its establishment, medium and large landowners received most of the credit supply in the agricultural sector. I was impressed by both the high repayment rate and the promotion of nonfarm employment in rural areas for men and women from the landless and near-landless households, who received nearly ten US dollars each. However, this notable progress needed the provision of marketing services and the promotion of new skills.

I gave my opinion to the development studies director. Briefly, my opinion was that if tenancy reforms were effectively implemented and the landownership ceiling lowered to six to eight acres, together with the strengthening of nonfarm employment and labor-intensive cropping, poverty in rural areas of Bangladesh would more likely be alleviated from its estimated high level of 75 percent (1980).

E. Russia

Certainly, and judging from my long experience, this trip to Russia, which was still officially part of the Soviet Union at that time, was an international tale. My visit in June 1991 originated with an invitation from the All Union Academy of Agricultural Sciences (Vaskhnil) of the Soviet Union at Moscow. I met one of its economists in Geneva, where he learned from the United Nations Research Institute on Social Development about my work on the political economy of market-based land reform. But Vaskhnil was unable to finance my mission, so they asked assistance from the European Economic Community (EEC) at Brussels. Vaskhnil wanted my advice on the individualization of collective land rights of farms administered by the old collective cooperatives, as well as on what to do with their state farms, the area of which was vast—nearly 215 million acres, representing 66.4 percent of the Russian total agricultural land in 1980, and employing 11.3 million workers. The aim of these proposed changes was to reform the centrally managed socialist agrarian institutions as part of President Mikhail Gorbachev's promarket reforms, which he initiated in 1988.

Without access to detailed microdata on each state farm, it was difficult for a foreign analyst like me to generalize on the Russian reform of the collectives and farms. These facts were difficult to obtain even from my field visits to a sample of collectives and state farms, during which I was under close supervision (even in my leisure time at the hotel and during my shopping). I was also faced with politicization and ideological bias with regard to such economic questions as decision making, economies of scale, labor remuneration, measuring efficiency in resources use and employment, marketing the farm products, production incentives, and so forth. Even worse was the reluctance of local staff to give me data they possessed, as well as the obvious language problems. My remarks and recommendations on policy matters were given in English and translated into Russian in a meeting of senior staff attended by nearly one hundred employees. This arrangement was against my wish to limit the attendance to senior economists of my host, Vaskhnil. However, throughout my one-month visit, I was impressed by the curiosity of both farmers and officials to learn about private property rights and duties associated with the large farms in a capitalist economy in the Anglo-Saxon countries. My explanation was simple: the institution of private property has been an essential part of democracy.

State farms, on the other hand, started in Russia in the 1920s as an integral part of the centralized authority of the state. The purpose was to provide the government with sufficient power over commanding food production, both to guarantee its supply for consumption by the large numbers of the armed forces and employees in the urban centers and to have an absolute command over larger-scale employment. I explained to my curious hosts that these privately owned large farms in the capitalist system are characterized by high output per person. For example, I told them that in the United States, Canada, New Zealand, and Australia, typical farms are managed by one family, even though they range in size between five hundred and two thousand acres. I explained that their high level of productivity per capita was the result of skilled owners, efficient management, and notable use of technology, supported both by substantial investment in research and, by extension, service. I also gave them an example of this efficiency in the United Kingdom and Egypt, around 1980, where labor in agriculture was 3 and 46 percent of the total labor force, respectively, but capital in the form of tractor per hectare was 77 and only 1, respectively. I added that in 1980, the median size of landholding was three hundred acres in the United Kingdom, compared with two acres in Egypt, and that the cultivator's real income per year was nearly a hundred times higher in the United Kingdom than in Egypt.

In my visit to Russia in 1991, I noted that the gigantic process of privatization of both collective (*Kholkhoz*) and state (*Sovkhoz*) farms was taking place and expected to be completed by 1992. It took longer than hoped for, owing partly to the fact that privatization of property and use rights included land, equipment, and buildings, and partly to the resistance to change by privileged classes in the giant political system of the Communist Party. Hence, the slow change of the economy from the powerful Central Committee toward capitalist market institutions. But the reader should know that the economic structural reform of Gorbachev had a clear political objective: breaking the power of the ruling Communist Party.

The rapid implementation of the 1990 Russian law on privatization began despite several difficult and complex changes that were required for the provision of a steady supply of food and agricultural raw materials for industrial activities. In this context, the process of privatization had to follow the central government's bureaucratic guidelines, particularly the legal aspects of property-rights transfer, which proved to be complicated.

This orientation toward the market economy was enhanced by President Boris Yeltsin's decree of January 1992 that legalized the retail and wholesale trade activities of middlemen. Nevertheless, I found that the supply of both credit and tractors continued to be far below what was planned. I was even told by Professor K. Khystan, chairman of the State Land Reform Committee, that the total procurement of grains by the state declined from 30 percent of the total grain crop in 1989 to 23 percent in 1992. The balance exhibits an increase in private sector trade. For readers who wish to learn more about Russian agrarian reform, I suggest *The Political Economy of Agrarian Reform in Post-Soviet Russia*, edited by D. V. Atta (1993).

CHAPTER 3

CREATING GLOBAL AWARENESS
OF RURAL POVERTY

3.1 Formulation of Socioeconomic Indicators for Monitoring Changes

In the early 1980s, in the Food and Agriculture Organization of the United Nations (FAO), I was able to establish an international working system for monitoring and evaluating progress in poverty alleviation via agrarian reform and rural-development programs. This work was in compliance with the demands of all FAO member countries and all UN agencies that adopted the recommendations of the World Conference on Agrarian Reform and Rural Development (WCARRD), held in Rome in July 1979. They agreed that the FAO should take the leading role within the United Nations system to collect, on a regular basis, relevant quantitative data for the purpose of establishing benchmarks for the years around 1980 and to report on progress made every four years. To accomplish this task, the FAO was required to assist statisticians and planners in developing countries in promoting their statistical programs to be used to monitor and evaluate rural poverty reduction and for policy analysis.

The FAO took five steps to meet this challenge:

1. establishing an interdepartmental working committee to adjust and coordinate activities within the FAO;
2. establishing a task force among UN agencies for the same purpose;

3. assisting the governments of developing countries in training relevant personnel in undertaking and understanding the monitoring procedures;
4. organizing regional meetings for the countries' statisticians and planners to reach a general agreement on the core of the indicators for estimating poverty and monitoring its reduction; and
5. testing the indicators in pilot work carried out in twenty-six countries (of which I participated in five: Cuba, Ecuador, Nepal, Mozambique, and Tunisia).

In this exploratory phase, I made a special effort to study India's long experience in conducting and analyzing poverty studies. Also, I had interesting discussions within FAO departments on undernutrition, malnutrition, food security for the poor, rural women and the level of disaggregation (rural versus urban, socioeconomic groups, sex, and age), land access, wage rates, current prices, and purchasing power. Out of this preparatory work, and with the assistance of the FAO Nutrition Division, I was able to define poverty in rural areas by emphasizing basic nutritional requirements.

Between 1981 and 1986, my work on making global rural-poverty estimates was expanded by the need to examine the minimum nutritional requirements for the survival of a *person* (instead of using the *household* as a unit) as the primary element in determining the poverty line. This question led to penetrating and illuminating discussions with Amartya Sen at Oxford University in 1985 with regard to his own research (Sen 1982), and to consult him on the plan for writing my book *The Political Economy of Rural Poverty*.

The Challenge of Measuring Undernutrition
As I stressed earlier with regard to nutrition and its close association with human health, I compiled available data on undernutrition and the absolute poor and undernourished. On examining these data on the relationship

between nutritional status and poverty, I discovered that the poor were not all undernourished (especially when income criterion is used for establishing a poverty line) but that the undernourished were almost always poor.

But who were those poor and undernourished in rural areas? On examining the country surveys and the FAO country tables for the period 1969–81, I found that they suggest the following categories for the rural poor:

1. small farmers in rain-fed areas that are unfavorable to sustained production of food;
2. hired agricultural (landless) workers in developing countries with a market economy reaching 180 million in 1985 (basic data in *Country Tables*; FAO 1987);
3. pregnant and lactating rural women; and
4. young children whose indicators of undernutrition are higher among girls than boys below the age of five.

I found also that considerable debate has arisen over whether absolute poverty is actual deprivation of particular basic needs in *physical* terms, or whether it should be measured generally in *monetary* terms, comparing income levels with some defined standard. An important distinction must be made between the actual deprivation of *physical needs* and the level of *purchasing power*. The former, measured by direct surveys, applies to people whose actual consumption, mainly of food, falls below a stipulated minimum requirement. The latter, extrapolated from limited household income/expenditure surveys, would apply to those whose income is insufficient to meet those minimum needs.

There are other problems. Consider a household with an income regarded as the minimum needed to meet all basic needs but that, for some reason or other, spends its income so carelessly that members of the household suffer from undernutrition. That household would not be poor using income as a measure; but measured in terms of food consumption or against anthropometric standards for children, the household would be undernourished and therefore "poor." In another example, the same level of nutrition can be provided by different combinations of food items. For instance, a diet based on rice or wheat may cost more than an equivalent one of millet and sorghum. There are also those who survive on naturally growing vegetation or on food aid. By the income method they would be very poor but not by the nutrition method.

Many countries use a poverty line to determine the number of households or individuals who are poor—that is, those, in physical or income terms, who live below the established level. In estimating a poverty line, some allowance is made for spending on nonfood items, such as clothing, housing, and fuel, as well as education and health. The latter group of items (education and health) is often provided or subsidized by governments to varying degrees, creating further problems in the measurement of poverty incidence. For example, if Country A provides more public services than Country B, the poverty lines in the two countries would be different despite otherwise similar conditions and prices.

Nutrition can be considered the most essential of basic needs—without adequate amounts of fuel, clothing, and education, people may continue to live, but without food they most certainly will not. Because of this, poverty lines have sometimes been defined in terms of food, and some scholars argue that poverty should be measured specifically in terms of undernutrition. However, the risk is that this would lead to an underestimation of the incidence of rural poverty because other basic needs are left out.

Evidence from India illustrates how the physical and income methods of assessing poverty each produce different results. Setting a "minimum income" based on nutritional requirements and basic needs at two hundred rupees per capita per year, one investigator estimated that the number of poor in rural areas fell from 46 percent of the total rural population in 1960–61 to 37 percent in 1967–68. Another survey, using a minimum-calorie requirement translated into money value, came to a completely different conclusion: because of rising prices, rural poverty increased from 38 percent in 1960 to 53 percent by 1968. Finally, a survey that used a minimum nutritional level of 2,250 calories per day as the poverty line found that the number living below it rose only slightly between 1960–61 and 1971–72, from 40 percent to 46 percent of the total rural population.

There are other issues in estimating poverty incidence. The question remains: How do we measure the incidence of absolute poverty within a population living below the poverty line? Do we simply add together all the people identified as poor, or is it preferable to take households as primary units and add together the number of households? For the purpose of this study, individuals rather than households are preferred. Therefore, the overall measure of rural poverty is expressed as the percentage of the poor in each country's rural population. Account may also be taken of the average income of the poor and of how far their incomes fall below the poverty line. All these issues involve the question of aggregation, which is controversial but cannot be avoided, because monitoring progress toward the alleviation or elimination of poverty requires measures for describing the severity of the rural poverty problem in each country. Depending on the level of aggregation, these measures may or may not be useful in the choice and execution of antipoverty programs and policies.

3.2 Characterizing the Land-Tenure Groups and Variations in Food Productivity

After identifying the landless agricultural workers, we can also ask, who are the "small farmers" who were repeatedly mentioned earlier? Despite the use of different definitions by different countries, some common characteristics emerge:

1. The size of the cultivated land area is smaller than the average in an agro-ecological zone.

2. The produce obtained is mainly for self-consumption.
3. The average income obtained is very close to the established poverty line.
4. There is little or disadvantaged access to credit.
5. The small farmers have little or no influence on how public decision-making affects their farming and living conditions. (For example, in 1974 India established its definition of *small farmers* as cultivators of 5 acres in dry-land areas or 2.5 acres of irrigated land; those below that size are termed *marginal farmers*.)

When I examined the results of various agricultural censuses since 1950, I found that

1. small landholders of less than two acres each (nearly one hectare) are the primary growers of grain in the world (75 percent of harvested wheat, 68 percent of rice, and 60 percent of maize or corn);
2. rural women are the most significant producers of food grain, livestock, and dairy products, yet they are virtually invisible to policy makers and technocrats in most developing countries; and
3. large landholdings were most prevalent in Central and South America.

A. Large Farms and Multinational Corporations

The foregoing section characterizes the prevalence and problems of the landless and the small farmers. I turn now to the opposite end of the spectrum and highlight the predominance of large farms, with emphasis on the plantations of multinational or international corporations. The focus is on these corporations' effects on wages and food production, as well as the trend toward increasing parceling and fragmentation, particularly as a result of inheritance rules and religion. Being familiar with the situation in Latin America, where I worked with the FAO for nearly three years (1958–61), I shall start this section with the large holdings situation in four countries:

Brazil, Colombia, Panama, and Venezuela. Then I examine the situation in Kenya, where I carried out an extensive field survey in 1993–94.

The purpose of both studies was to create awareness of the linkages between poverty levels and the degree of landholdings concentration in Latin America and in Kenya, using the results of the agricultural censuses in 1970 and 1980. In Brazil, the share of one thousand hectares and over in the total number of landholdings in 1971 was only 0.8 percent, but its share in total cultivated areas was high, at 40 percent. In Colombia, it was 0.2 percent and 31 percent respectively. Venezuela was even worse: 1.7 percent and 68 percent respectively. According to the 1985 *World Development Report*, per capita income level, measured in US dollars per annum, was $658 in Brazil, with Venezuela much higher at $1,553. My compiled data on rural-poverty estimates show that the percentage of the rural population living in *absolute poverty* in 1980–81 was as follows: Brazil, 67 percent; Panama, 30 percent; and Venezuela, 56 percent (despite its high level of per capita income for 1982).

My analysis of these estimates and the data on landholdings distribution suggests the following high degrees of association:

1. The higher the land concentration, the higher the poverty incidence in rural areas.
2. The share of large-size landholdings is strikingly stable over the two periods of the study in the 1970s and 1980s.
3. Despite high average per capita income, poverty in rural areas is very high, suggesting gross inequality in the distribution of assets and income as well as widespread deprivation in rural areas.

With regard to the African situation, my 1992 field study on Kenya's large farms and poverty incidence revealed that before Kenya's independence in 1963, the British settlers expanded their area in the *highlands*, thereby creating a dichotomy in the agricultural sector where small Kenyan farmers and nomadic populations live in the *lowlands*. A distinction between highlands and lowlands in the cropping pattern was obvious: high-value cash crops (tea, coffee, pineapple, and tobacco) were grown in the highlands, encouraged by concessions, exemptions, and incentives, whereas food crops (maize, millet, sorghum, cassava, and sweet potatoes) were grown by Kenyan small farmers. I also examined an old colonial project (the million-acre land-settlement scheme), which allocated part of the white settlers' area of highland plantations to native Kenyans in small plots. Accordingly, 1.2 million acres were purchased by the natives at market value from large plantation owners, whose area of landownership reached 6 million acres, with the right of the plantation owners to transfer the sale value abroad free of tax. Nevertheless, landholding concentration continued.

According to my examination of the results of the 1981 agricultural census in Kenya, of the total number of holdings in the small-farm sector, 83 percent were less than two hectares (nearly five acres). At the other extreme, I found that the large-farm sector (including multinationals and British plantations) held 2,129 farms with a total area of 2.6 million hectares. Approximately 81 percent of these farms were over two hundred hectares each, 930 of which were five hundred hectares each, compared with the average two hectares for native Kenyan farmers. After Kenya became independent in December 1963, large plantations like Del Monte continued on, and private foreign capital vigorously responded to the government investment program (providing investment protection through the Finance Act of 1964), which also provided large farms with several exemptions. Many of these farms became partners with native Kenyan capitalists in agricultural development (joint ventures), whereas other multinationals like Unilever maintained a high market share in the control of poultry production, vegetable fat, dairy products, tobacco, and medicinal plants. I also found a new class of large landowners in Kenya, many of whom were members of parliament and cabinet ministers. In the meantime, the government lifted institutional barriers for small farmers to grow cash crops (tea, coffee, pyrethrum, sisal, and sugarcane). Accordingly, labor use was intensified on these small farms.

B. Small Farms and Their Fragmentation

My professional interest in creating awareness about and raising the alarm on the impact of the prevalence of fragmented small holdings on the productivity of both land and labor (including the landholder), and in turn the distribution of income, have induced me to conduct relevant country case studies. Apart from Egypt, which was the focus of my PhD study during 1952–54, my investigation covered Libya, where I was the FAO supervisor of a large rural-development scheme for the resettlement of formerly Italian farms before Libyan independence in 1951. Thereafter, my interest continued in Algeria, Morocco, and Tunisia. In 1976 I presented the results of my field studies at a regional meeting of the ministers of agriculture and their senior staff from these three countries.

The meeting discussed the following development issues:

1. the variation in land-productivity levels by the size of holdings;
2. the share of different size classes in the total food production;
3. the causes of land fragmentation, including Islamic inheritance principles; and
4. whether the fragmentation has constrained or contributed to food production.

The term *small holding* was used as defined in the countries' own agricultural censuses. The meeting recognized that, in principle, the prevalence of small holdings should not bring about adverse effects, because small farms intensify the use of both land and family labor. That is, they should have a much higher degree of resource use and cropping intensity percentage-wise than large farms.

On examining the causes of the division of landholdings into separate small plots, my 1962 empirical studies in Egypt and Morocco show the following contributing factors:

1. population pressure on land;
2. many small landholders tending to rent in additional areas, in separate plots;
3. international migrants using their remittances to attract small landholders to sell parcels of their land;
4. rapid urbanization and the construction booms; and
5. inheritance arrangements that require splitting up the deceased's landownership into several parcels among heirs after meeting debts and funeral expenses (the size of distribution of mandatory shares, or *naseeb*, differs according to sex and the religion of the landowner and inheritors).

Sudan and Darfur: A Case of Aggressive Neglect

The results of my field studies and the material presented during the discussions held in Tunisia were donated to the Queen Elizabeth House's Library at Oxford University. Encouraged by the support received from senior government officials in Tunis in 1976 and by the invitation received from the governor of Sudan's huge Gezira project, I pursued my examination of the root causes of poverty and the famine in 1984–85 in Darfur and Kordofan, the two large provinces of Sudan. The tangible causes were very low rainfall in 1981–82 followed by the severe drought in 1984–85, which brought about the "Famine That Kills" (de Waal 2005). In Darfur alone it was reported that ninety-five thousand people and 55 percent of their livestock died. In addition, these events caused chronic undernutrition among children. I also donated the material collected during my field studies in Sudan to the library at Queen Elizabeth House at Oxford.

I also studied the Sudanese government's expanded irrigation-pump scheme, the establishment of a large-scale settlement of Khashm el-Girba in 1964, and the small Undokono scheme for the settlement of some nomadic pastoralists. During my subsequent field visit in 1974, I found that many of these Sudanese settlers had no experience in growing cotton and groundnuts, which they were obliged by the government to grow. Also, I found that nearly one-third of the settlers were absentees and their land was cultivated by hired workers, which contradicted the rules of the scheme. The settlers were also grouped into heavily patronized cooperatives, cultivating their lands under strict government control and confusing bureaucratic rules. The upshot was a lack of coordination among three separate departments (irrigation, agriculture, and local government), resulting in high administrative costs that I estimated at 26 percent of the gross value of output per land unit.

I wish to remind the reader that at the time of my Sudanese field study, famine occurred in five other African countries (Mauritania, Senegal, Upper Volta, Niger, and Chad), where the number of human deaths was estimated at one million. Also, Ethiopia experienced severe famine in 1973–74 that killed nearly one million people. Here again, the international agencies' explanation was generalized and confusing: the decline of food availability, a general shortage of food, a sharp rise in prices of rice, the dependence on rainfall without sufficient investment in irrigation, and so on. Interestingly, Sen (1981, tables 9.5 and 9.6) documented that the FAO and other sources of official data indicated that in 1974–75, the year of Bangladesh's famine, per capita availability of food grains and the total supply of food grains for consumption were sufficiently high.

Looking back to these sad events, we are fortunate indeed that the development issues of undernutrition, poverty, starvation, and famine have been the focus of analytical research; some of them have already been cited above. Others include Kevin Cahill (1982), who has written about famine;

Godfrey Tyler (1983) on Somalia; and Eileen Egan (1995) on the role of voluntary nongovernmental organizations.

Clashing Views of Political Economy: Comprehensive versus Fragmentary

In 1987 the University of Reading invited me to give a series of lectures to officials from developing countries interested in such questions as how to define the poor and what development approaches would be most successful in alleviating poverty.

My lectures were followed by my presenting a paper for discussion at the Annual Conference of the Development Studies Association held at the University of Birmingham. The title of the paper was "The Distortion of Rural Development Issues." As I saw it, the "distortions" occurred on the part of governments after the introduction of structural and market-oriented agricultural and rural-development policies influenced by the World Bank and donor countries. Many saw these proposed policies as mere window dressing that avoided the core elements of land tenure–based institutional monopoly.

Like that of Reading, the Birmingham conference was attended by many academics as well as government directors of field programs. In both meetings I examined the consequences of ignoring the social aspects of development issues as formulated by the founders of social philosophy and political economy during the eighteenth and nineteenth centuries. These prudent founders (Adam Smith et al.) refrained from separating analytical reasoning from actual empirical observations on the social organization of economic phenomena operating within the laws and customs of society in which they lived. Hence, they did not ignore such customs and institutions as inheritance and land-tenure arrangements, which are habitually ignored by contemporary neoclassical economists. We know that the founders of economics—Adam Smith, David Ricardo, John Stewart Mill, and Karl

Marx—had clear vision and a comprehensive understanding of the issue. They were concerned about economic phenomena embedded in the age-old feudal land-tenure systems in Britain and Ireland and the institutional arrangements of sharecropping in France and parts of Europe in their day.

I also explained at both Reading and Birmingham the rise of the marginal-cum-mathematical analysis of economics in the nineteenth century and the leap of neoclassical economics in the last century. Consequently, the comprehensive understanding of the complex sociopolitical forces in shaping development has been broken up into separate, narrow areas of concern. Accordingly, economics as one branch of social science has been divided into theoretical and applied disciplines. Also, the theoretic apparatus has, therefore, distanced itself from political economy that is based on elements of social organization and shifted toward the static equilibrium of physical-commodity relations. As viewed by Gordon (1965) and Coats (1969), economics has become dominated by a "single paradigm of maximization of resource allocation via the market forces."[3] On separating economics from noneconomic aspects, Joan Robinson of Cambridge University said in her *Aspects of Development and Underdevelopment*, "Western teaching pretends to be scientific and objective by detaching the economic aspects of human life from the political and social setting; this distorts the problems that it has to discuss rather than illuminating them" (Robinson 1979, 3).

Empirically, I examined the negative consequences of partial understanding of development issues in my analysis of the results of my field studies on the impact of agrarian structural changes in Kenya, South Korea, Paraguay, Brazil, and the Philippines. In my field investigation of

---

3   See A. W. Coats (1969), "Is There a Structure of Revolution?" cited in Ranadive *Income Distribution: The Unsolved Puzzle*, Oxford University Press, p. 331. See also El-Ghonemy, M. R. (1990), "The Puzzle in the Analytic Reasoning behind Policy Prescription" in *The Political Economy of Rural Poverty*, and Gordon, D. (1965), "The Role of the History of Economic Thought in the Understanding of Modern Economic Theory," *American Economic Review*, pp. 19–27.

development economics in practice, I highlighted that the misleading con-clusions, history, and social organizations were *separated from* economic growth, income distribution, and people's participation—through their own organization in the development experience of these five countries. A comprehensive development apparatus was used in the analysis of my field observations, the results of which are published in my two books (El-Ghonemy 1990 and 2010).

During the period 1988–93, I continued employing this comprehen-sive analytical approach of realism in development economics when pre-senting the experiences of Algeria, Egypt, Libya, Morocco, and Tunisia in my book *Land, Food and Rural Development in North Africa*.

3.3 Responding to the Increasing Demand for Understanding the Market's Role in Poverty Alleviation

In the 1990s, I was engaged in responding to several international events concerned with the subject of poverty reduction amid the increasing in-fluence of the World Bank and the IMF on developing countries. These two institutions encouraged the adoption of their market-based economic reforms, including fiscal and trade liberalization—that is, free of govern-ment intervention. These events included grand (and perhaps grandiose) international conferences and "summits."

1. The 1992 International Conference on Nutrition held in Rome indicated that
    a. only 40 percent of the total cereal production is consumed by people and the rest is consumed by livestock and reserved as seeds;
    b. although data on national and world averages of food con-sumption are useful indicators, they do *not* show *actual* human food intake; and

   c. 786 million people were chronically undernourished or hungry in 1992, one-third of them in Africa, and the world average was estimated at 20 percent.

2. The 1996 World Food Summit set the goal of halving the number of the undernourished by 2015.

3. The 1995 World Summit on Social Development held at Copenhagen, established the goal of *eradicating* poverty and *eliminating* undernutrition.

4. The Development Assistance Committee of the Organization for Economic Cooperation and Development (OECD), in its meeting in Paris in 1996, set the goal of halving the proportion of the poor by 2015.

5. The September 2001 UN General Assembly Millennium Development Goals included halving the proportion of poverty and the people suffering from hunger between 1990 and 2015.

I should remind the reader of two other major events: the early 1990s collapse of the Soviet Union—a nation that had been a strong supporter of government intervention and development objectives for rapid reduction of inequalities and poverty—and the World Conference on Agrarian Reform and Rural Development (WCARRD), which was held in Rome in 1979 and agreed to *eliminate* undernutrition by the year 2000 because of world leaders' beliefs that poverty, hunger, and malnutrition retard national-development efforts and negatively affect world social and proeconomic stability.

In my book *The Crisis of Rural Poverty and Hunger*, I made a critical assessment of all these conferences' resolutions, indicating their generalities and ambiguities with regard to poverty and undernutrition measurements. I focused also on the most unlikely realization of the goal "halving poverty/undernutrition by 2015." To the contrary, I explained with statistical evidence the likely prospect for increasing the incidence of both, in addition to effects of possible natural disasters like severe drought, armed conflicts, and civil unrest.

A major factor entering this debate was the rising influence of the post-1985 shift in development goals away from government intervention in the market mechanism (demand/supply and wages/prices) and vigorously toward liberalization in production and trade, with greater powers to the private sector irrespective of negative distributional effects. This sudden post-1985 development perception was hurriedly implemented in developing countries, with inducements by the World Bank, the IMF, and the rich Western economies, starting with the heavily indebted poor countries. I examined this shift in policy perception and development objectives with emphasis on its impacts on poverty and food production in chapters 7 and 8 of *The Crisis of Rural Poverty and Hunger*.

In that book, I argued that this standard perception would most likely increase poverty and inequality in asset ownership and income distribution.

I gave empirical examples of my case studies on government-administered redistributive land reforms in Egypt, Iraq, Mexico, and South Korea compared with market-based land policy in Brazil, Colombia, Kenya, and the Philippines.

For an illustration, let us explain what happened in Brazil, whose land-concentration index (Gini) was as high as 0.63 in 1992 and where rural poverty was also high at 73 percent. To pacify the millions of poor peasants and landless workers, the government of Brazil passed a law in 1985 to redistribute private land. But it was not implemented. Instead, using loans from the World Bank and the International Fund for Agricultural Development (IFAD) and supported by the Federation of Agricultural Workers and university representatives, a new market-based program was initiated, whereby landowners could sell parts of their properties to the peasants, who purchased land using the loans financed at easy terms.

However, I learned during my field study that the plan was met almost immediately with difficulties. The absence of land and taxation (cadastral) surveys, combined with the landowners' sale of very low-production land at high prices, resulted in making this attempt a disaster. In addition, serious administrative difficulties were compounded by violent conflicts between the occupants of the land and its owners. I also discovered that all these negative factors have led to less than 6 percent of the total landless agricultural workers in Brazil (estimated at 1.4 million) acquiring land.

Similar results were observed during my field study, in 1990 in the Philippines, of land transactions under the market forces initiated in 1996 by President Ramos, which enabled the tenants to purchase the land they till. This program was financed by the World Bank and the Ford Foundation. Their funds and efforts were frustrated and even defeated by a combination of the erstwhile clumsy bureaucracy and the overvaluation of land prices under the local monopoly powers of the landlords. I was able to examine this situation in March 1990, when I was invited by the Institute of Agrarian Studies of the Philippines University. What happened was that the landlords and the powerful multinational corporations opposed the program and wanted the government to concentrate on the distribution of state-owned land and the land voluntarily offered by landlords for sale at market value. I noted also the almost complete absence of land-property registration and land taxation. Furthermore, several landowners told me that the government should not interfere in the transaction of land both for lease and for sale. Later, I learned that the net result in 1999 was that *only 7 percent* of the land area targeted in 1990 for property transfer was realized.

Another feature of market-based change was the *privatization of customary land*, which I examined in Malawi, Sudan, and Uganda during 2002. I presented the results in Arusha (Tanzania), Nairobi, and Dar-el-Salam. This privatization of customary land took place despite strong arguments for maintaining customary land tenure, including those arguments of the World Bank itself, and despite of a lack of hard evidence on the production superiority of private/freehold/individual tenure over customary communally owned land. This sort of privatization policy under neoliberal reforms is vigorously pursued in some Latin American and many African countries. It is also enforced in spite of empirical evidence that the secure and inheritable customary tenure system is as compatible with the production of export crops as with food production. It is also compatible in production incentives and risk reduction.

The findings of available studies in Malawi, Kenya, Uganda, and Sudan suggest that individualization of customary land has led to the vulnerability of individual owners to the loss of land property by sale to larger landowners and urban land speculators, as well as by mortgage as a result of heavy indebtedness.

After these negative impacts of the sweeping post-1985 market-oriented policy, the World Bank has lately acknowledged, from accumulated empirical evidence on the impacts of individualization and formal titling of customary land tenure, that (1) benefits from land titling are not enough to justify the costs of conducting land-title investigation and land registry; and (2) private titling of land is not a realistic alternative to communal tenure. Nevertheless, it may take decades to unravel the tangled web of what have been, in my opinion, misguided policies.

CHAPTER 4

EXAMINING THE DETERMINANTS AND CONSEQUENCES OF EXTREME INEQUALITIES IN THE MIDDLE EAST

4.1 The Wide Variation in Natural-Resource Endowments

G uided by the results of my field studies in five North African countries, prepared for the International Fund for Agricultural Development (IFAD) in Rome, I was able to determine the causes and consequences of the prevalent degree of inequality in the distribution of assets, including education, natural resources, and income in these countries. This feature of inequality has clearly emerged in my investigation of "The Standard of Living in Egypt" in *Egypt in the Twenty-First Century* (El-Ghonemy 2003). In that study, I examined the effects of historical, environmental, and globalization linkage. My analysis of available data on country and household consumption provided by income/expenditure surveys conducted between 1958 and 2000 indicated growing disparities and their unfavorable health-related and other social effects. I also estimated *social costs* defined as the sum of money required for the restoration to the original state—that is, before the occurrence of unfavorable change.

In my seminars and writings, I have conceptualized this state of existing extreme inequality. I examined the roots and consequences of flagrant inequality in the distribution of wealth, income, and opportunities for employment. *Wealth* is defined in these two occasions as exchangeable physical and financial assets, as well as personal skills including education and the ability to bear risk and establish connections that generate income. In judging inequality, I assumed that individual income distribution is more unequal than household income, which is a pool of individual income. I also highlighted, for welfare purposes, the principle that specification of expenditure is essential for understanding the consumption components (food, education, clothing, transport, leisure/luxury expenditure, and so on). In my lectures, I pointed out the importance of understanding the influence of political and social institutions on the economic factors that determine inequality between and within the different income groups. Examples of these historical and institutional factors are colonialism (or foreign political/military occupation) and the sociology of class stratification (or the determinants of class status).

The reader may have noticed my frequent emphasis on how ownership of land determines income and political and social power. It is crucial how wealth is accumulated and used. I make this point because affluence is often used synonymously with abundant wealth, property, flow of money, and extreme riches or opulence. We should remind ourselves that the founders of the field of economics reckoned that opulence meant "the possession of wealth," hence the important gross and per capita national incomes. In turn it has been, and still is, believed that high rates of growth and greater opulence tend to eliminate poverty over time. *But after how long?*

In the debate that followed my presentation of seminars in Egypt in 1998 at the Ramses Hilton hotel and Ain Shams University, questions were raised. For example, why the emphasis on income as a single measurement, when there are such important alternatives as health and education? Another point was that what is necessary or basic in a country may not be the same in another (owing to such variations as climate and culture).

However, the discussion has shown a general agreement about the importance of the individual's nutritional status, reflecting a combination of

his or her health, education, and lifestyle, and in turn, food security or insecurity, fear, and submission by individuals and countries. It was also agreed
among the discussants that country case studies, including of historical
roots, are more meaningful for policy design than a reliance on world aver-
ages and estimates provided by the World Bank, UNICEF, ILO, and FAO.

My seminars and writings have suggested that a distinct and clearly
perceptible feature of the existing extreme inequality in the Middle East
region is manifested in the wide variation in natural-resource endow-
ments—oil, water, and cultivable land—while their shortage is increasing
under population pressure. Given the arid nature of most of the region's
land and the countries' limited capacities to invest in water conservation
and irrigation expansion, I explained this long-term development challenge. I also highlighted the fact that meeting this challenge depends on
the degree of scarcity per both locality and time.

Furthermore, it depends on the rate of extraction of such exhaustible
resources and on government policies, combined with public awareness,
particularly in the Gulf States where oil is concentrated. These two deter-
minant factors (rate of extraction and government policies) are important
for a number of reasons.

First, the Middle East possesses just less than half of the estimated
world oil reserves, nearly 80 percent of which are concentrated in the Gulf
States.

Second, the estimated oil-extraction time remaining is relatively short
in Algeria and Libya (30 years from 1994) but much longer in Saudi Arabia
(60 years), Kuwait (150 years), and Iraq (135 years) from 1994.

Third, oil wealth is concentrated in a few countries. Saudi Arabia holds
almost one-fifth of the region's total reserves and produces about 12 percent of the world's total. Likewise, Algeria possesses the fourth-largest gas

reservoir in the world and annually produces 27 percent of the gas production of the region.

Fourth, as the Middle East region is in the arid and semiarid climatic zones of the world, nearly 53 percent of its total population live in areas with less than the acceptable minimum level of a thousand cubic meters of water per person. What is more alarming is that availability of water per person in the year 2000 was only one-third of its 1960 level, and if present rates of use continue, the average is expected to halve by 2025. Such an increasingly diminishing water supply, combined with the rising competition for water use between agriculture, industry, drinking, and other domestic purposes, necessitates country and collective regional actions for rational water use and the conservation of existing agricultural land, not only to feed the growing population but also to prevent further desertification and famines. Alas, like the downward trend in water availability, all indications suggest increasing land degradation and desertification by way of water logging, salination, topsoil loss, deforestation, and overgrazing. Poor countries (Sudan and Mauritania) and the poorest rural households are most affected by the worsening situation. This downward trend gives cause for concern, given the increasing dependency of the Middle East region on food imports (including food aid) and given that the poor are the most vulnerable to food-insecurity risks.

4.2 Oil Windfalls: From Poverty to Sudden Affluence

Around 1940, Libya and Saudi Arabia were among the poorest of the underdeveloped countries. Within a tribal organization, more than half their population were nomadic or seminomadic Bedouin. Their economies were chiefly dependent on grazing, camel raising, growing cereals when rainfall permitted, fishing, and exporting sheep, hides, and dates. In addition, Saudi Arabia relied upon pilgrimage revenues, roughly estimated at US$20 per person. To illustrate how poor Libya was, its government was unable to initiate the first development program *without* external donations. Not so long ago, between 1954 and 1958, grants to Libya from the United States, the United Kingdom, France, Egypt, and Turkey, together with the United Nations' assistance, represented nearly half the Libyan government's total revenue. To illustrate further the sudden oil-based affluence, Egypt and Lebanon in the 1930s and 1940s were much advanced relative to Saudi Arabia and Libya in terms of income per person, educational level, health services, physical and institutional infrastructure, advanced industrialization, and strong linkages with world trade. In 1939–40, income per person in Egypt was estimated at US$60 compared with approximately US$30 in Saudi Arabia, US$35 in Kuwait (in 1945), and US$40 in Libya. Among all Arab countries, Lebanon was at the top, with its income per person at US$140 in 1949.

4.3 Unprecedented Pace of Wealth Accumulation: Libya, Saudi Arabia, and Kuwait

Unprecedented windfall gains followed the discovery of petroleum by foreign companies and their investment in its extraction and export both in Saudi Arabia (1944–50), and in Libya (1959–62). Accordingly, the average annual income of a Saudi rocketed in a short period of only five years, reaching a level in 1962 that was forty times higher than in 1957; it had risen a further fourteenfold by 1970. The most dramatic jump was between 1979 and 1981, when oil revenue almost doubled in only two years. In Libya the jump was even greater. To the best of my knowledge, human history has *not* previously experienced such a scale of affluence gained in such a short period of time. For instance, in less than twenty-five years, Libya had reached an average annual income of US$7,170 per person in 1985, a level of GNP per person that had taken the currently rich industrialized countries 220 years (1750–1970) to attain. With such sudden, rapid affluence, the lucky governments of the oil-rich states were so overwhelmed by the flow of plentiful oil revenues that nearly three quarters of their countries' natural-gas wealth (a by-product of crude petroleum) was *wasted*.

In my book *Affluence and Poverty in the Middle East* (1998), I indicated how between 1960 and 1991 oil increased intercountry inequalities in income, stock of international capital reserves, and, in turn, opportunities for progress. Countries are ranked by the 1991 GNP per person, which would not fundamentally change if we were to use the new estimates of GDP based on purchasing power parity (PPP) in international dollars for 1990. This change, made by the UN Statistical Office, indicates how much of each country's currency is required to buy the same amount of goods and services in the domestic market as one dollar would buy in the United States. According to these new estimates, the ranking order of the Middle East countries would result in Egypt's higher ranking above Morocco, the classification of Jordan above Syria and Tunisia, and of Turkey above Algeria and Iran. Whichever income concept is used, Sudan, Yemen, and Mauritania remain the poorest countries. The unanticipated jumps in wealth and income originate in the pace of the oil price boom, which was in sharp contrast to the sluggish trade in such nonoil minerals as phosphates in Morocco and Jordan, which are among the world's five largest producers of this commodity.

Considering the low cost of oil production per barrel in the Middle East, the price boom of the 1970s has brought a sudden high economic rent (profit) to a few governments and particular ruling families. Stauffer (1987, 30) estimated this windfall gain at nearly 80 percent of the price of each barrel. Perhaps no other exportable primary commodity produced in the region (such as cotton, sugar, tobacco, and phosphates) has included in its price so high an element of profit. Furthermore, oil-windfall gain has accrued with little productive effort on the part of society. Internationally, a significant indication of the emerging power of oil money were the loans of US$10 billion granted in 1981 by Saudi Arabia to the IMF and US$800 million to the World Bank when commercial creditors in the Western countries were so weakened by recession that developing countries had almost no access to international borrowing.

Instead of directly helping needy countries, the Saudi loan enabled the IMF to respond to their acute needs.

Against a background of deprivation and foreign command over their oil industry, the now oil-rich governments and the ruling families received either the full economic rent or a contract rent resulting from the nationalization of the oil industry, which began in the Middle East in 1953 by Mohammad Mosaddeq, the then prime minister of Iran. Accordingly, payments by oil companies to governments greatly increased between 1950 and 1975: by 1,700 times in Libya, by 658 times in Kuwait, and by 240 times in Saudi Arabia. A manifestation of their sudden affluence is the sharp rise in gold holdings and in vast reserves of foreign exchange, facilitated by keeping a large stock of wealth in the industrialized countries of the West in the form of gold and financial assets (such as bond issuances and shares).

According to international financial statistics produced by the IMF, Saudi Arabia's gross international reserve, including official gold holdings, jumped by 133 times between the average for 1958–62 and the average for 1980–85. The average reserves per person (including gold) in Saudi Arabia rose sharply between these two periods by a factor of nearly seventy, with the reserves per person in the United Arab Emirates being the highest in the Middle East. Iran also tended to favor holding gold in international reserves; the weight of Iranian gold in ounces was greater than that of both Kuwait and Saudi Arabia. Likewise, Libya, which was classified by the United Nations in 1950 as a poor, underdeveloped country, had in 1980 the highest value of international reserves per person in the Middle East, US$4,969 (including gold). This is an extremely high level of affluence compared with that of the rich industrial countries, such as US$753 in the United States and US$566 in the United Kingdom. However, I contend that these criteria for ranking are misleading. Oil-rich Arab states are developing countries with a high degree of economic dependence on external forces outside their own control. They are also characterized by underdeveloped institutions and infrastructures, as well as by an extensive social and economic imbalance. Moreover, the GNP of the six rich Arab states *combined* was equivalent to only 7 percent of the United States' GNP and was nearly one-third of that of the United Kingdom in 1980, when oil revenues peaked.

In absolute terms, the total income (GNP) of a single country, Saudi Arabia, was US$438 billion in 1991, which exceeded the total income of seven countries: Egypt, Jordan, Mauritania, Morocco, Syria, Tunisia, and Yemen, whose collective population numbered 145 million, represented 43 percent of the region's total population at that time. Although the income gap between the richest and poorest nations widened between 1960 and 1980, it narrowed slightly in 1991, after the oil slump of 1981–86. Mismanagement of oil windfalls in the rich countries during the boom (1974–80) and the good growth performance of the region's poorer countries were both contributing factors in this. In 1980 a person in the United Arab Emirates or Qatar had, on average, an annual income that was sixty-three times greater than that of a person in Sudan or Yemen.

4.4 Sharing Oil Windfalls: Financial Aid and Worker Remittances

My assessment of the affluence in the Middle East is incomplete without mentioning the clarification that I made in my seminars at Egypt's Ain Shams and the University of Tanzania. For various motives, rich Arab states have transferred substantial sums of oil money to poorer countries directly through untied financial aid and indirectly by way of migrant workers' remittances. Between 1973 and 1990 nearly US$50 billion was unconditionally provided for poorer Arab states and Turkey, mostly in the form of bilateral and concessional assistance (almost grants). In addition, I presented in these seminars my estimate of an amount of US$88 billion being transferred by migrant workers to their Arab home countries during the same period. In terms of its proportion to national income (GNP), financial aid from rich Arab states has, since the sharp rise in oil prices of 1973, exceeded the UN target of 0.7 percent and the average of rich industrialized donors (0.3 percent). It was high at 5.9 percent in 1973–74 and fell steadily to 1.8 percent in 1990 and 0.8 percent in 1991. Saudi Arabia is the largest donor by far. Its share in total Arab financial aid jumped from 51 percent in 1973 to 75 percent in the 1980s. In terms of aid per head of the population of donor countries, Qatar and the United Arab Emirates surpassed Saudi Arabia.

One would expect that this sizable transfer of oil money from rich Arab donors would have effectively contributed to human development and poverty alleviation in poorer recipient countries if—and I emphasize *if*—it had been directed to activities that diminish poverty directly. Alas, nondevelopmental considerations, especially military spending, have been so dominant that financial aid can hardly be classified as development assistance. In retrospect, this was a missed opportunity for the recipient countries' emancipation of their people from deprivation. To appreciate this point, consider the fact that the Arab aid of US$50 billion was more than three times the sum of US$14 billion given in the US Marshall Plan during 1947–52 for Western Europe's speedy recovery from the devastation, hunger, and poverty caused by the Second World War. It seems that both Arab donors and recipient countries lacked the sort of vision and development-oriented leadership of such statesmen as Harry Truman, George Marshall, and Dean Acheson of the United States, and Clement Attlee, Ernest Bevin, Charles de Gaulle, and Conrad Adenauer of the recipient European countries during 1947–52.

I should remind the reader that financial aid after the military defeat of Egypt, Jordan, and Syria in their 1967 war with Israel was encouraged and mandated by the heads of Arab states in their summit meetings, and the exact size and timing of disbursements were usually kept secret from the public. Unlike the financial assistance from rich industrial countries, no system of surveillance exists between Arab donors and recipients. One possible explanation is the almost complete absence of democratic machinery for accountability and for monitoring both the allocation and the effects of disbursed bilateral financial aid.

EPILOGUE

T hroughout this book, I have maintained that the ultimate responsibility for antipoverty-policy choice rests with the sovereign governments of the developing countries. Yet external factors do influence
that choice, particularly since the world economic problems of the 1980s
(mounting problems of debts, inflation, trade, and balance of payments
deficit). These economic factors led to diminishing foreign assistance
by rich donor countries (members of the Organization for Economic
Cooperation and Development, particularly the United States, United
Kingdom, and Germany). The power of their large shares in capital stock
and their significant voting power in this international funding agency
cannot be underestimated.

According to this post-1980s ideology, the market, *not* government intervention only, is the effective means of alleviating poverty. But under
which institutional systems of transactions and legal framework can the
market and related incentives work in developing countries? When the
distribution of both income and accessible opportunities is grossly skewed,
the market works for the benefit of traders, large and medium farmers,
and multinational corporations, while most probably harming the landless
agricultural workers and poor peasants.

In my two books *The Political Economy of Rural Poverty* and *The Crisis
of Rural Poverty and Hunger*, I have clarified a common misinterpretation
of "for" or "against" government intervention and "pro" or "anti" market

approach *without* specifying a focus on poverty reduction or on the nature of government intervention. It is equally unhelpful to make a generalized policy preference between "market-based" and "state-based" (or administered/mandated) land reform without placing the debate in a country-specific agrarian context. For example, South Korea's initial agrarian conditions made it necessary for that country's leadership to pursue, since the 1950s, a complete land-reform policy combined with rural nonfarm-employment expansion and substantial human-capital investment. In addition, institutional arrangements provided and supported the market toward greater exports and investments in priority areas. Moreover, the South Korean government has guided the market toward economic stability by such measures as setting an effective exchange rate and interest rate and promoting exports. Like South Korea, Japan and Taiwan (of the Republic of China) carried out, in the late 1940s and 1950s, extensive redistributive programs combined with the introduction of government regulations that enabled the market mechanism to gradually function effectively.

One should ask the following question: In the absence of government intervention in these countries, what would have happened to the reduction of rural poverty and inequality and to the sustained economic growth that brought about the superior economic performance described by the World Bank in 1993 as the East Asian Miracle? This *complementarity* between government activism and market-assisted policy at an early stage of development is behind these countries' current superior economic performance. Whether land-tenure reform is politically feasible under certain power structures is not for the social scientist or the development analyst to judge. What these professionals can do is use their faculties and professional tools to understand the totality of rural underdevelopment problems in a specific situation; to analyze the determinants; to point out implications of these determinants for poverty, equity, economic growth, and conflicts of interest; and to suggest alternatives.

Throughout *The Political Economy of Rural Poverty*, I argued that *land reform is the alternative* to a state of rural underdevelopment characterized by skewed distribution of land, income, and accessible opportunities as well as by falling food productivity. I have also argued for the effective participation of the rural people through their own representatives. Motivated nongovernmental organizations (NGOs) with the support of committed middle-class intelligentsia can help mobilize national support for programs of antipoverty and the removal of injustice in society. Still, organized participation faces enormous barriers. Many governments either prohibit the very existence of agricultural trade unions, while allowing them in nonagricultural sectors, or render them powerless through denying their rights (Palmer 1983).

The effectiveness of nonstatutory organizations is enhanced by occupational or gender homogeneity among their members. For example, women, who constitute almost half of the agricultural workers in many developing countries, have traditionally been excluded from village organizations, trade unions, and agricultural cooperatives, whose membership has been the prerogative of men. With the exception of socialist countries, rural women are rarely given titles to land in land reform and settlement schemes. This hardworking silent majority have been, and still are, denied their legitimate rights in land and to influence the design of policies and programs to reflect the realities of their high rate of participation in the total labor force.

I have emphasized the fact that the ultimate aim of policy makers in developing countries is to increase the productivity of the poor and to realize social stability by means of effective participation of the poor, who neither know how to lobby nor how the political system of their countries is organized. Finally, I leave the reader with one question to ponder: Given the foregoing analyses, has the lot of the rural poor improved significantly over the past sixty or so years?

Bibliography

Abu-Zahra, M. 1963. *Ahkam al-tarika wal-mawareth* [Teachings of inheritance]. Cairo: Dar el-Fikr el-Arabi.

Adelman, I. 1974. "South Korea." In *Redistribution with Growth*, edited by H. Chenery, M. Ahluwal, B. Bell, and R. Joll. Oxford, UK: Oxford University Press.

———. 1987. *Practical Approach to Development Planning*. Baltimore, MD: Johns Hopkins University Press.

Baumol, W. J. 1965. *Welfare Economics and the Theory of the State*. London: Bell and Sons, Ltd.

Cahill, K. 1982. *Famine*. Ossining, NY: Orbis Books.

CAPMAS, *Statistical Yearbook*, several years. Cairo.

Cleaver, K. M. 1982. "The Agricultural Development Experience of Algeria, Morocco, and Tunisia: A Comparison of Strategies for Growth." World Bank Staff Working Paper 552. Washington, DC: World Bank.

de Waal, A. 2005. *Famine That Kills: Darfur, Sudan*. New York: Oxford University Press.

Egan, E. 1995. *For Whom There is No Room: Scenes from the Refugee World*. New York: Paulist Press.

El-Firgani, N. 1984. *Al-higra ela al-naft* [The migration to oil]. Beirut: Center for Arab Unity Studies.

El-Ghonemy, M. R. 1953. "Resource Use and Income in Egyptian Agriculture Before and After Land Reform." PhD diss., North Carolina State University.

———. 1954. "Rural Labour-Disguised Under-Employment." Field study presented at the annual conference of ILO, Geneva.

———. 1965. "The Development of Tribal Lands and Settlements in Libya." *Land Reform.*

———, ed. 1967. *Land Policy in the Near East.* Rome: FAO.

———. 1968. "Land Reform and Economic Development in the Near East." *Land Economics* 44 (1): 36–49.

———. 1968. "Economic and Institutional Organisation of Egyptian Agriculture Since 1952." In *Egypt Since the Revolution*, edited by P. J. Vatikiotis. London: George Allen and Unwin.

———. 1979. *Agrarian Reform and Rural Development in North Africa and the Near East.* Cairo: FAO Regional Office for the Near East.

———, ed. 1986. *The Dynamics of Rural Poverty.* Rome: FAO.

———. 1987. "Why Development Economics Has Suffered a Relapse in the 1980s." Seminar given at Cornell University, Ithaca, NY.

———. 1990. *The Political Economy of Rural Poverty: The Case for Land Reform.* New York: Routledge.

———. 1992. "The Egyptian State and Agricultural Land Market: 1810–1986." *Journal of Agricultural Economics* 43 (2): 175–90.

————. 1993. *Land, Food and Rural Development in North Africa*. Boulder, CO: Westview.

————. 1998. *Affluence and Poverty in the Middle East*. New York: Routledge.

————. 1999. "The Political Economy of Market-Based Land Reform." Discussion Paper 104, United Nations Research Institute for Social Development, Geneva.

————. 1999. "Food Security in North Africa." In *Economic Development*. Vol. 1 of The Political Economy of the Middle East, edited by T. Niblock and R. Wilson. Cheltenham, Gloucester, UK: Edward Elgar.

————. 2000. "Mafhoom wa tatawor al-tanmiya al-rifiya fi Misr: al-dorous al-mostafada wa tahadiyat al-mostaqbal" [Evolution of rural development concepts and experience in Egypt: lessons learned and future challenges]. Lecture given on March 22, 1998 at the Conference Hall of the Ramses Hilton, Cairo, published in Arabic in the conference proceedings by the National Commission for Population and Development, El-Maadi.

————. 2001. "Dor al-islah al-mo'assassi fi isr-aa al-tanmiya" [The role of institutional reform in accelerating development]. Seminar given in March, Ain Shams University, Cairo.

————. 2002. "The Land Market Approach to Rural Development." In *Agrarian Studies*, edited by V. K. Ramachandran, Vikas Rawal, and Madhura Swaminathan. New Delhi: Talika Books.

————, ed. 2003. *Egypt in the Twenty-First Century: Challenges for Development*. London: Routledge.

―――. 2003. "Land Reform Development Challenges of the 1960s Continue into the Twenty-First Century." *Land Reform Journal* 2003/2 (December).

―――. 2007. *The Crisis of Rural Poverty and Hunger: An Essay on the Complementarity between Market and Government-Led Land Reform for Its Resolution.* Routledge Studies in Development Economics. London: Routledge.

―――. 2009. "Al-gha'eb min ihtimamina bel-amn al-ghiza'ee" [The absent issues from our understanding of food security]. *Al-Ahram Al-Dawly* newspaper, section on development issues, May 14, Cairo.

―――. 2010. *Anti-Poverty Land Reform Issues Never Die: Collected Essays on Development Economics in Practice.* Routledge Studies in Development Economics. London: Routledge.

El-Wifaty, B. 1978. "Evaluation of Land Settlement Programs in Libya." Mimeographed copy, Study, FAO Regional Office for the Near East.

Faisal Islamic Bank. 1979. *Faisal Islamic Bank: Its Objectives and Operational Methods.* Khartoum: Faisal Islamic Bank.

―――. 1983. *Report of the Board of Directors.* Khartoum: Faisal Islamic Bank.

FAO. 1983. *Review of Food Consumption Survey 1981.* Study for the FAO. Rome.

―――. 1985 and 1990. *Country Tables: Basic Data on the Agricultural Sector.* Rome: FAO.

Feder, G., and A. Nishio. 1998. "The Benefits of Land Registration and Titling: Economic and Social Perspectives." *Land Use Policy*, 15(1): 25–43.

Feder, G., and R. Noronha. 1987. *Land Rights Systems and Agricultural Development in Sub-Saharan Africa*. Washington, DC: The International Bank for Reconstruction and Development/World Bank.

Ghai, D., C. Kay, and P. Peek. 1988. *Labour and Development in Rural Cuba*. The ILO Study Series. Washington, DC: Macmillan.

Gombya-Ssembajjwe, W., A. Y. Banana, and J. Bahati. 2001. "Explaining Deforestation: The Role of Forest Institutions in Ugandan Forests." A Policy Brief. Kampala, Uganda: Ugandan Forestry Resources and Institutions Center-Makerere University.

Hayek, F. 1986. *The Road to Serfdom*. London: Routledge.

Higgins, B. 1959. "Economic Problems and Policies in Libya." Washington, DC: World Bank.

Hirschan, A. D. 1981. *Essays in Trespassing Economics to Politics and Beyond*. Cambridge, UK: Cambridge University Press.

International Labour Organization. 1983. *Rural Labour Market Issues*. Geneva: ILO.

Islam, R. 1985. "Poverty, Income Distribution and Growth in Rural Thailand." In *Poverty in Rural Asia*, edited by A. R. Khan and E. Lee. Bangkok: ILO and Bangladesh Institute of Development Studies.

Issawi, C. 1947. *Egypt: An Economic and Social Analysis*. Oxford, UK: Oxford University Press.

Leite, T. 1994. "Reform and Development in Brazil, Working Paper No. 176." The Hague: Institute of Social Studies.

Manghas, M., and B. Barros. 1980. *The Distribution of Income and Wealth*. Manila: Philippine Institute for Development Studies.

Marshall, A. 1952. *Principles of Economics*. 8th ed. London: Macmillan.

Marx, K. 1906. *Capital: A Critique of Political Economics*. New York: Modern Library Edition.

Mathews, R. C. O. 1986. The Economics of Institutions and the Sources of Growth." *The Economic Journal* 96 (December): 903–18.

Mellor, J., and G. Desai, eds. 1985. *Agricultural Change and Rural Poverty*. Baltimore, MD, and London: Johns Hopkins University Press.

Ministry of Agriculture. 1988. *The Results of the Agricultural Census of 1981–1982*. Cairo.

Myrdal, G. 1960. *Beyond the Welfare State*. New Haven, CT: Yale University Press.

———. 1968. *Asian Drama: An Inquiry into the Poverty of Nations*. New York: Twentieth Century Fund.

Oakley, P., and P. Marsden. 1984. *Approaches to Participation in Rural Development*. Geneva: ILO.

Otsuka, K., and F. Place, eds. 2001. *Land Tenure and Natural Resource Management: A Comparative Study of Agrarian Communities in Asia and Africa*. Baltimore, MD: Johns Hopkins University Press.

Palmer, I. 1983. *The North-East Rainfed Agricultural Development in Thailand: A Baseline Survey of Women's Rules.* New York: Population Council.

Peek, P. 1984. *Collectivising the Peasants: The Cuban Experience.* Geneva: ILO.

Perkins, D., and S. Yusuf. 1984. *Rural Development in China.* Baltimore, MD: Johns Hopkins University Press.

Ranadive, K. R. 1978. *Income Distribution: The Unsolved Puzzle.* Oxford: Oxford University Press.

Ravallian, M. 1987. *Markets and Famine.* Oxford: Clarendon Press.

Rawls, J. 1973. *A Theory of Justice.* Oxford: Oxford University Press.

Robinson, J. 1969. *Economics of Imperfect Competition.* London: Macmillan.

———. 1979. *Aspects of Development and Underdevelopment.* Cambridge, UK: Cambridge University Press.

Roemer, J. E. 1982a. *A General Theory of Exploitation and Class.* Cambridge, MA: Harvard University Press.

———. 1982b. "Exploitation, Alternatives and Socialism." *Economic Journal* 92 (March): 87–107.

Russell, B. 1938. *Power: A New Social Analysis.* New York: Norton.

Ruttan, V. W. 1984. "Integrated Rural Development Programmes—A Historical Perspective." *World Development* 12 (4): 393–401.

Safilos-Rothchild, C. 1982. *The Persistence of Women's Invisibility in Agriculture: Theoretical and Policy Lessons from Lesotho and Sierra-Leone.* New York: Population Council.

Schultz, T. W. 1981. *Investing in People: The Economics of Population Quality*. Berkeley: University of California Press.

Sears, D. 1969. "Challenges to Development Theory and Strategies." *International Development Review* (December): 2–6.

Sen, A. K. 1964. "Size of Holding and Productivity." *Economic and Political Weekly*. Vol. 16, No. 2: 323-26.

———. 1975. *Choice of Techniques: An Aspect of the Theory of Planned Economic Development*. 3rd ed. Oxford, UK: Basil Blackwell.

———. 1981. *Poverty and Famine: An Essay on Entitlement and Deprivation*. Oxford, UK: Clarendon Press.

———. 1983. "Development: Which Way Now?" *Economic Journal* 93 (December): 745–62.

Singer, H., and J. Ansari. 1982. *Rich and Poor Countries*. London: George Allen and Unwin.

Smith, A. 1937. *The Wealth of Nations*. New York: Random House. First published 1776.

Sobhan, R. 1983. *Rural Poverty and Agrarian Reform in the Philippines*. Poverty Studies 2. Rome: FAO.

Southall, R., ed. 1988. *Labour Unions in Asia and Africa: Contemporary Issues*. London: Macmillan.

Stauffer, T. 1987. "Income Measurement in Arab States." In *The Rentier State*, edited by H. Beblawi and G. Luciani. London: Macmillan.

Stigler, G. 1982. "The Economists and the Problem of Monopoly." *American Economic Review* 72 (2): 1–11.

Streeten, P. 1972. *The Frontiers of Development Studies*. London: Macmillan.

———. 1981. *Development Perspectives*. London: Macmillan.

Streeten, P., S. Burki, M. ul Haq, N. Hicks, and F. Stewart. 1981. *First Things First: Meeting Basic Needs in Developing Countries*. Oxford: Oxford University Press.

Szal, R. 1984. "Trends in Income Distribution in South Korea and their Relationship to Policy and Planning." In *Towards Income Distribution Policies*, edited by H. P. Nissen. European Association of Development Research and Training Institute Book 3. Tilburg: Tilburg University, Netherlands.

Taylor, L. 1977. "Research Directions in Income Distribution, Nutrition and the Economics of Food." *Food Research Institute Studies* 16 (2): 29–45.

Todaro, M. P. 1981. *Economic Development in the Third World*. 2nd ed. New York: Longman.

Toye, J. 1987. *The Dilemmas of Development*. Oxford, UK: Blackwell.

Tyler, G. J. 1983. *Somalia: Case Study on Rural Poverty*. Poverty Studies 7. Rome: FAO.

Tyler, G. J., and A. Khan. 1986. *Yemen Arab Republic: Rural Development Strategy and Implementation*. Report of the United Nations ESCWA Mission. Baghdad: ESCWA/FAO Agriculture Division.

UNICEF. 1984. *Statistics on Children in UNICEF Countries*. New York: UNICEF.

United Nations Centre on Transnational Corporations. 1983. *Transnational Corporations in World Development*. New York: United Nations.

Wan Dong, S., and C. Yang-Boo. 1984. "Alleviation of Rural Poverty in the Republic of Korea." Rome: FAO.

Wheeler, D. 1980. "Human Resources Development and Economic Growth in Developing Countries: A Simultaneous Model." World Bank Staff Working Paper 407. Washington, DC: World Bank.

Wickramasekara, P. 1985. "An Evaluation of Policies and Programmes for the Alleviation of Poverty in Sri Lanka." In *Strategies for Alleviating Poverty in Rural Asia*, edited by R. Islam. Bangkok: ILO.

Williams, S., and R. Karen. 1985. *Agri-Business and the Small-Scale Farmer*. Boulder, CO: Westview.

World Bank. 1978. *Thailand: Toward a Development Strategy of Full Participation*. Bangkok: World Bank East Asia Regional Office.

———. 1980. *Aspects of Poverty in the Philippines: A Review and Assessment*. 2 vols. Washington, DC: World Bank.

———. 1983. *Focus on Poverty*. Washington, DC: World Bank.

———. 1984. *Social Indicators Data Sheets*. Washington, DC: World Bank.

———. 1984. *World Development Report, Development Indicators*. Washington, DC: World Bank.

———. 1988. *World Development Report*. Washington, DC: World Bank.

INDEX

ABOUT THE AUTHOR

From his birthplace of Delingat, a poor village in the Nile Delta of Egypt, M. Riad El-Ghonemy began his long journey and career as a development economist by earning a coveted scholarship that enabled him to attain a PhD in the United States. He then worked with the Food and Agriculture Organization (FAO) of the United Nations for twenty-eight years, where he helped the poor worldwide achieve a better standard of living. Since retiring from the UN, Dr. El-Ghonemy's life has been dedicated to academia and to writing books and articles based on his global experience. He is an elected honorary lifetime associate at the Department of International Development at Oxford University. He divides his time between his residences in the United Kingdom and Egypt.

Website: www.riadelghonemy.com